Open this book. Look inside.
death with her. Choose life
resilience and creative brillia. ... *young woman stood*
naked before each broken piece of her heart only to discover in their
reflections the true colors of her soul. These pages weave a tapestry just
as her grandmothers have always done, one sacred dyed thread at a
time. Death was the portal. Writing was her blessed balm. And a life of
love carried her from magic into madness into a mature ministry. Let
her bravery be a balm to your aching heart. Risk everything for love.
Sarita has. She lights the way, serving as a teaching for all who wish to
befriend our deepest fears and greatest longings.

—Melissa Michaels, Ed.D., founder of Golden Bridge and
Surfing the Creative; Author of *Youth on Fire: Birthing a*
Generation of Embodied Global Leaders

You hold in your hands a work of true heArt. We are given the gift,
and pain, of witnessing the journey of a human who loved and lost
more deeply than most of us can ever can imagine. She has taken the
wounding of immense destruction and woven exquisite beauty. And, at
the end of it, Sarita gives us not despair but rather, an awe-inspiring
Hope. She opens our hearts to the understanding that the canyons of
grief and the rivers of praise that run through us are one and the same.
It is a story that sings the pieces back together: in her journey the most
magnificent phoenix is born from the ashes. I wish for every human
to read this book, whether or not you have survived the unthinkable.
My wish for you is to take in it's medicine. To lift the words from the
page and whisper them to your soul. To breathe deeply and let your
marrow crackle with the wisdom alchemized by disaster. By addressing
our greatest wishes and our deepest fears, Sarita teaches us that our
hearts can be "broken wide open with love.

—Summer Steele, poet

Sweet Water
TSUNAMI

Nicolás Butí,
Harrysito de mi corazón,
Amor de mi vida,
GRACIAS
Es todo para vos…

Published by Golden Bridge
PO Box 7478
Boulder, Colorado 80306

Printed in the United States of America

Cover and layout design by Chelsea Jewell
Edited by Earl Jon Rivard Jr.

ISBN: 978-0-692-97793-4

Sweet Water Tsunami—A praise, a thank you, a wish

Sometimes a thing comes through the thickest fog and reminds you that you have a heart. And not only that, but a heart that lives among other hearts.

Sweet Water Tsunami came to me in a black binder on a rainy day in a trailer in Colorado. It came to me over tea and stories swapped and through a shared understanding of how the things you think are everything, shatter.

I took the binder home with me, an unfinished manuscript, and for two months it was a wellspring in the desert. It was not my story and was entirely its own and still it soothed and rocked and raged and fumbled through the dark beside me like nothing else could. In a time where both my grief and my love was mostly still, scared to come out and still layered in the shock of my changed world, the poems and prayers and wails of Tsunami melted the tears frozen behind my eyes and brought voice to the tangle in my throat that longed for prayer. It lit a fire where there had not been light for a long time and reminded me with a certain quiet ferocity that life goes on.

For those two months the words of *Tsunami* became a song. They were the broken lullaby that put me to sleep at night—a voice rough and true rising up out of a broken heart that could not be replaced by anything sweet or smooth or whole. Their bitterness let me breathe, told me I was no more crazy than the world, and wrapped me up with the wily kind of knowing that is only born out of the depths and the edges.

You see, the words in this book are the kind that will catch you writhing in the dark and lock eyes with you and whisper into your ear "I know." They will say it over and over until you settle back into your skin and remember that it is night and that something new might come with the morning. The story in this book is one and only, and yet its uniqueness is bridged by an unwavering understanding of the prayer that comes through all torn hearts: That beauty may persist and crack open every story that would like to prove otherwise. That the burning to create that wakes you up in the night and the words scrawled half-legible on the page in the dark that might not hold water for half of the people who read them—that they will save your life, and perhaps one day, someone else's.

And so to anyone that finds themselves bending over these pages—

Drink. Let this be honey for what is tired in your soul. It will meet you where you are most cracked, tell those parts they are true, and then light a match so that there might be something else, also.

If this book is a light, then it is a light that has learned respect for the dark.
If this book knows beauty, then it knows ugly just as well.
If this book is a will toward trust, then it is a will grown out of shatteredness.

These are the things that let me hold it close.

Cantando al sol, como la cigarra,
después de un año bajo la tierra,
igual que sobreviviente que vuelve de la guerra.

~ *María Elena Walsh*

Table of Contents

KINDLING FOR THE FIRE

On March 15th, 2013, my beloved life partner, soulmate, and best friend, Nicolás was suddenly taken by death.

All light disappeared, the future vanished. All impulse, all dreams, were swallowed whole.

Nothing of me was left. Nothing of what I knew on this strange planet applied. I died as well.

Now, I tiptoe through this waking nightmare, following the scent of remnants of myself strewn like breadcrumbs on the path.

Piece by piece, I re-collect and re-member. staggering forward, howling for grace to find me again.

Below the deafening static of a hemorrhaging heart, an ancient whisper calls me to re-assemble the bones of my soul.

To survive by transcribing this living death.

To tell the story that will sing the pieces back together again.

To glean from my descent some small treasure to share with others who have been cut by this dangerous dance on thin ice, and are still here, living into the mystery…

Art is my temple, my teacher, and my therapy.

A sacred expression of words and tears and paint and life-blood is within reach, is reaching for me…

The veil is thin; I am broken wide open, and in order to heal, something must be born of this. Something must give birth to me. Something with the power to transform this pain…

Preface

I wrote this book all at once,
as if possessed,
in a craze in the desert.

I wrote it to save my life.

Six months after the unthinkable happened,
I did what any crazy person would do,
and I bought a Colombian machete from a street vendor
and went out into the desert,
to a nearly abandoned adobe house, four kilometers from town.
To write.
It was a bingeing, or a purging, I am not sure.

I wrote this book because I had to.
In five swift months, I lost and found myself to the sacred and
gory ritual of hemorrhaging onto the page. I cannot say the
bleeding stopped, but something of these words are my coagu-
lated life force, somehow returned to me by giving it to, being
witnessed by, the story.

And in the three years after my time in the desert, I could not
touch it.

I waited for a sign of how it should be "finished." I continued
grieving, and continued living. I even continued loving, and all
the while I waited for the insight on how to somehow make it
presentable, coherent, neat, tidy, logical.

I waited for the final ah hah! For the discernment of pruning
shears, or the new bloom that would finally fill it out, make it good,

…Make it o.k.

I waited to be "o.k."...

I waited to be able to give testament to a full bloom after being seared to the root. I wanted to make it a story about hope, and resilience. I wanted to give my readers some gold at the end of the dark tunnel that was this initiation.

And as I waited, I stepped around the shyly printed and rarely read manuscript, kicking it further and further beneath my nightstand, until it eventually became a secret diary rusted under lock and key.

I have tried to go back in with an editor's mind and somehow tame the madwoman and crown the architect of the story, nail the pieces together in a way that makes sense.

But nothing about this writing makes sense, nor is it solid. It was written while hanging from the snagged fabric of the veil.

When I re-visit this writing, it is as if I am reading it for the first time. It's as if it were not I, but rather a ghost or a glimmer of me, that wrote it.

I have no right to go back in and manipulate it in order to make it right.
It is just right.
It saved my life.

What is done is done. A fossilized snapshot into the hell realms, a holy re-membering of truth.

And I sometimes question if that was not its full purpose.
Does it need to be shared?

Perhaps, it is not intended for those who are in their right minds.

Perhaps it is too cryptic, chaotic, incoherent to be fully accessible to those of us who are walking with our feet planted in the land of the living.

I am doing the final push of making this madness accessible to the world with the slightest hope that it may reach someone who is tethered to their Body by a single strand of splintering sinew.

This book was written from that realm, and maybe could reach someone calling themselves home, and maybe my wailing will somehow bring comfort or comradery to someone who is feeling like an alien, who would much rather be dead.

If this is you, I wrote this book for you…
If this is not you, I ask you to bear with me, and to bear witness to me. And I invite you to make space for the aching places in you that you may not wear on your sleeve, for the Grief AND for the Praise that is the heartbeat of our loves and of our lives…

…May it become medicine, May it be so…

Este hombre, Hombre de mi Vida.
Fuerte, alegre, simple, auténtico, profundo, pleno, pícaro,
apasionado y puro.
Palabras sabias,
Sonrisa contagiosa de payaso,
Besos de chicle, de miel, de dulce de leche, de nubes y ángeles y
olas del mar.
Mi Barrilete Cósmico,
Mi Mejor Amigo,
Mi voz de la razón en momentos de duda.
Mi Consuelo, mi Inspiración, mi Bendición, mi Tesoro, mi SOL.

Hermano leal, generoso y protector.
Admirador y alumno de quienes lo merecían.
Tío tierno,
Jugando al Oso Yogi,
Eligiendo vestiditos coloridos en el mercado extranjero.
Infinitamente paciente, generoso.
Ejemplo humano de compasión y de comprensión.

Amigo fiel, siempre dispuesto, positivo, presente.
Jodón, timbero, Fernecero, kilombero, pininicero.
Pateando la pelota, rompiendo las pelotas.
Aventurero, pescador, carpintero, artesano, malabarista, futbolista,
Este hombre callaba el ruido de la sobremesa con sus argumentos
inteligentes, coherentes, educados, y justos.
Respetado y querido, aclaraba con solo ser, regalándonos su
liviandad refrescante, su confianza convincente.
Alegrando lo que tocara, con su don de disfrutar.
Es él, quien nos anunciaba la noche en pañales,
El, quien oraba con voz callada, humilde y transparente de shaman,
El, quien le ponía leña al fuego,

El, quien nos mostraba el camino, con pasos livianos y lúcidos.
Este hombre daba todo por el amor.
Entregado con una esencia más noble que la inocencia,
Ganándome con B*on-o-Bones*,
Parchando mi bici pinchada, con rodillitas barrosas y boquita
de Nesquick.
Presumiéndome con vueltitas en el boliche y tragos helados de
la barra.
Conquistándome con su gracia para el dia-a-dia,

Con su integridad, su manera de ser, de estar, compartir y cumplir.
Parecía ser sin esfuerzo su lucha, su trabajo, su compañerismo y
su compromiso.
Este hombre, este Excelente Hombre era un gigante.
Tan grande era, que el orgullo de ser su mujer se me desbordaba,

El agradecimiento de recibir su amor me endeudaba,
La alegría de compartir la vida con él, me iluminaba.
Al lado de mi Rey, fui La Reina, descalza, despeinada, adorada
y descubierta.

Este Hombre, con valentía de león.
Dispuesto a luchar por lo que amaba su corazón,
Sin razón, sin pretenciones, sin dudas, sin miedo.
Amante milenario, tierno, apasionado, fuerte.
Le salían chispas al verme encendida,
Y lágrimas al oírme llorar.
Pintando un arcoiris en mis pestañas empapadas,
Sacando risas de lo oscuro y de lo absurdo.
Al servicio de nuestros sueños, hasta el fin del mundo…

Este Hombre, de carcajadas en la cocina fría.
Momentos simples y sagrados de la convivencia cotidiana,

Surfeando livianamente mis enojos juveniles, mis caprichos, y nuestros reencuentros.

Lavando los platos entre besos robados.

Cantándome al oído en susurros, bailando lento.

Tecito con miel en días de lluvia,

Salta negra y maní picante en noches pesadas de luna amarilla y grillos.

De la mano en la terraza, mirando las estrellas.

Tardes anaranjadas de mate amargo, tortillas quemadas, y delirios intelectuales.

Descubriendo callejones exóticos en tierras extrañas,

Cartas de amor, poesías sagradas, fiestas descontroladas.

Leyéndome en voz alta, mi carita refugiada en su pecho.

Desayunos juntos, contentos y callados.

Brindando y agradeciendo con cada jugo de naranja, vino tinto, soda, Mirinda o chai.

Noches enteras, sentados en un banco de nuestra placita,

Desenterrando las raíces y disfrutando los frutos,

Podando lo seco, regando lo fértil, confesándonos y comprometiéndonos

Conspirando y planeando, cumpliendo y festejando.

Este hombre, sol de la mañana,

Ojos fogosos, observadores, profundísimos, ventanas al paraíso...

Mirando el mundo girar con curiosidad y con reverencia.

Viéndome, entera, mis defectos y mi gloria, y aceptándome.

Aceptando esta vida.

Aceptando lo que tocara, a pesar de lo feo, de lo herido, de lo no deseable, de lo no planeado.

Cultivando, invitando, y alabando el misterio creativo que danza entre mi vientre y el polvo de las estrellas.

Recordándonos siempre que de ahí venimos, y ahí volveremos...

Este hombre,

Mi Shaman, mi Hermano, mi Madre, mi Padre, mi Hijo,
mi Hermano,
Mi Mejor Amigo, mi Maestro y mi Gurú.
Mi canción preferida,
Lo más bello que he tocado.
Lo más bello que me tocó…
El regalo más inmenso que he recibido fue
Este hombre,
Escuchándome, entendiéndome, deseándome, mimándome,
malcriándome,
Acurrucándome, aliviándome, inspirándome, apoyándome,
aconsejándome,
Gozándome y alimentándome.

Su misión era hacerme feliz.
Y lo hizo.
Este hombre me hizo enormemente, extáticamente,
eternamente feliz.

No me digas viúda, con tono apenado.
Soy la mujer más afortunada del mundo.
Fui la mujer más feliz del mundo.
Viví lo que todos desean, y recibí lo que nadie se imagina…

Este hombre me comprobó la magia de los cuentos de hadas.
Truenos en mis rodillas, relámpagos en mis pulmones,
Mariposas en mi panza, y luciérnagas en mis ojos.
Me sanó con manos de curandero, me abrigó con calor del
amanecer.
Me bañó con amor divino, luz dorada que no se vence ni
desaparece.
Me maduró el corazón, guiándome en el desenvolver, mostrán-
dome su capacidad.

Me dio fuerza y fe, libertad y contención.
Me enseñó de la amistad incondicional.
Me inició en los misterios del amor puro,
En el arte de ser canal del amor, y del servicio desinteresado.
Este hombre le dio sentido a lo absurdo.
Fue cordura para este rompecabezas, este misterio mundano.
Me dio un hogar en esta tierra extraña.
Les dio aliento a mis sueños.
Me hizo volar.

Hombre de mi Vida,
Amor eterno de mi corazón,
Nuestra sagrada unión de almas entrenzadas es contrato
irreversible.
Sobrevive la fragilidad de esta materia.
Estás conmigo.
Estás impreso en mi ser...
Tesoro más precioso de la tierra y del cielo,
Dejaste huellas aquí.
Estás con nosotros...
Ni nada ni nadie nos puede quitar semejante bendición.

Aún con estas rodillas moretoneadas, con estos ojos salados, con
esta cara hecha charqui,
Con esta melena joven pero plateada, con estos sueños abortados,
Y con este corazón polvorizado,
Doy gracias por este hombre.
Demos Gracias por este hombre.
Doy Gracias por Harry.
Gracias, Mi Amor.

THIS MAN

This man, Man of my Life.
Strong, happy, simple, authentic, deep, full, clever, passionate and pure.
Wise words,
Contagious clown smile,
Bubble gum kisses, honey, caramel, clouds-and-angels and sea-wave flavored kisses.
My Cosmic Kite,
My Best Friend,
My voice of reason in times of doubt.
My Consolation, my Inspiration, my Blessing, my Treasure, my SUN.
Loyal brother, generous and protective.
Admirer and pupil to deserving elders.
Tender Uncle,
Playing Yogi Bear,
Picking out colorful little dresses in the foreign market.
Infinitely patient, generous.
Human exemplar of compassion and of understanding.

Faithful friend, always ready, positive, present.
Joker, gambler, drinker of Fernet, rouser of the rabble, *pininicero*.
Swinging a leg at the ball, pulling everyone else's leg.
Adventurer, fisherman, carpenter, artisan, juggler, *futbolista*,
Traveler, cook, tease, man of sincerity.

This man silenced the after-dinner babble with his insights.
Intelligent, coherent, educated, and just.
Respected and beloved, he clarified with his very being, gifting us his refreshing lightness, his convincing confidence.
Bringing happiness to all he touched, through the art of enjoyment,
It was he who rang in the night's festivities,

He, who whispered the shaman's humble, transparent prayer.
He, who added fuel to the campfire.
He, who showed us the way with light, lucid strides.

This man gave everything for love.
Giving of himself with an essence more noble than innocence,
Winning me over with *Bon-o-Bones,*
Fixing the flat on my bike, with muddy knees and a mouth
stained by Nesquick.
Seducing me with dance-floor spins and cold drinks from the bar.
Conquering my heart with his everyday grace,
With his integrity, his way of being, of sharing, of showing up
and stepping up.
His effort, his labor, his camaraderie and his commitment… he
made it all look so easy.

This man, this Excellent Man, was a giant.
He was so big that my pride at being his woman overflowed me,
My gratitude for receiving his love indebted me,
My joy in sharing his life illuminated me.
At my King's side, I was The Queen, barefoot, disheveled, adored
and brought to light.

This man, with the courage of a lion.
Willing to fight for what his heart treasured,
With neither reason, nor pretense, nor doubt, nor fear.
Millenary lover, tender, passionate, strong.
Sparks flew from him when I was alight,
As did tears when he saw me cry.
Painting a rainbow on my dripping lashes,
Milking laughter from the dark and from the absurd.
At the service of our dreams, beyond the ends of the earth…

This Man, of boisterous laughter in the frigid kitchen.

Simple, sacred moments of daily life,
Surfing, lightly, the flow and ebb of my tantrums, my capricious pouting, our reconciliations.
Washing dishes between stolen kisses.
Whispering songs in my ear, slow dancing.
A little tea with honey on rainy days,
Dark beer and spicy peanuts on humid evenings bathed in yellow moonlight and crickets.
Holding hands on the rooftop, watching the stars.

Orange afternoons, sipping bitter *mate* to go with burnt *tortillas* and wandering, euphoric wonderings.
Discovering exotic alleyways in unfamiliar lands,
Love letters, sacred poems, wild parties.
Reading to me out loud, my face nestled in his chest.
Shared breakfasts, contented and quiet.
Toasting and giving thanks with every glass of orange juice or red wine, every sip of sparkling water, *Mirinda*, or chai.
Whole nights spent sitting on a bench in our little plaza,
Digging up the roots and enjoying the fruits,
Pruning the deadwood, watering the fertile, making confessions and commitments,
Planning, conspiring, following through and celebrating.

This man, my morning sun,
His deep, deep eyes, passionate, observant, windows to paradise…
Watching the world spin with curiosity and reverence.
Seeing all of me, in my defects and in my glory, and accepting me.
Accepting this life.
Accepting whatever came our way, no matter how ugly, how wounded, how undesirable, how unplanned.
Cultivating, inviting, and praising the creative mystery that dances between my womb and the stardust.
Reminding us always that we are dust, that unto dust we shall return…

This man,
My Shaman, my Brother, my Mother, my Father, my Son, my Brother,
My Best Friend, my Teacher and my Guru.
My favorite song,
The most beautiful thing that I have touched.
The most beautiful thing to touch me.
The greatest gift I have received was

This man,
Listening to me, understanding me, desiring, caressing and spoiling me,
Cuddling me, relieving me, inspiring, supporting, and counseling me,
Enjoying me and nourishing me.

His mission was to make me happy.
And he did.
This man made me enormously, ecstatically, eternally happy.

Don't call me widow, with pity in your voice.
I am the most fortunate woman in the world.
I was the happiest woman in the world.
I lived what everybody wants, and I got what nobody can imagine…

This man proved to me the magic of the fairy tales.
Thunder in my knees, and lightning in my lungs,
Butterflies in my belly, and fireflies in my eyes.
My illness melted in his healer's hands, he cloaked me with the warmth of a sunrise.
He bathed me with divine love, golden light that neither diminishes nor vanishes.
He ripened my heart, guiding me and showing me its potential.

He gave me strength and faith, freedom and containment.
He taught me about unconditional friendship.
He initiated me in the mysteries of pure love,
In the art of being a conduit of love and of selfless service.
This man made sense of this absurdity.
He brought sanity to the quandary of this mundane mystery.
He gave me a home in this strange land.
He breathed life into my dreams.
He made me fly.

Man of my Life.
Eternal love of my heart,
The sacred union of our intertwined souls is an irreversible pact.
It outlives the frailty of this substance.
You are with me.
You are branded on my being…
Most precious treasure of heaven and earth,

You left your imprint here.

You are here with us…

Neither anyone nor anything could take such a blessing away.
Even with these bruised knees and salted eyes and face dried out
like jerky,
With this head of hair, silvered though young, with these aborted
dreams,
And with this heart blown to dust,

I give thanks for this man.
Let us give thanks for this man.
Doy Gracias por Harry.

Thank you, My Love.

WORDS

I knew that I needed to write. When I knew nothing. When all coherence and all constructs had crumbled, the spiritual and the solid, I knew only that I needed to write. What I did not realize is that telling this story is an impossible task.

Some of the writing is so belligerent, it will never be read by anyone, except by, maybe, a baffled therapist, if I can ever afford one.

Or perhaps it will be by a fifty-six-year-old me, searching for clues, who someday opens the unedited chronicles of the hell realms I have traversed, excavating the mystery of my unconscious during my next Saturn return.

There is writing, important writing, that is not meant to be shared, and there are stories too precious to whisper. There are shards of my shattered interior that have never slipped past my clenched teeth into the air, and that perhaps never will.

Maybe they will eventually be polished by my swallowed tears into a glistening cave of crystals in my throat.

Perhaps they will be forever painful, aching like a prosthetic hip when the weather changes abruptly.

And some parts I will never write, but will sometimes tell in hushed whispers, as if to conserve their soft forms, like breath on cold glass.

They are inexplicable, mysterious and fragile.

I do not tell the whole story to the whole, because this tapestry of crooked lines — ineffable, unnamable, immeasurable — unravels when tethered to words; because I fear I might tear the fibers of the spider web.

Undoubtedly, the medicine is not in the words on these pages, but in the very act of writing them. Nonetheless, I have attempted here to put into words an experience for which there are no words.

The depth of my pain is unfathomable.

The blessing of Harry in my life is indescribable.

The magnitude of this love and loss is unutterable; it is beyond any set of syllables, any pre-constructed symbols available to our language.

I have struggled wildly with the impotence of my own words, with the fear of dishonoring this story with my limited vocabulary, and, worst of all, I have wrestled with the danger of cheapening my experience by attempting to recount it. Surely, the pen *is* mightier than the sword. I might add, however, that the pen cannot scratch the surface of what the soul has endured. There is no way to convey what he has given me, or what losing him has taken from me. There is certainly no way to describe that which cannot be taken.

Luckily for me, and for all the artists who have attempted and failed to catch this unattainable butterfly in a jar, attempted and failed to do the impossible, to do it justice… some things do not depend on words to be communicated. To be woven from straw into gold. To be translated from stardust onto paper. Some things simply live at the very core of our humanness. Certain things our species has had the cruel and sacred privilege of experiencing since the beginning of time.
Such as finding divine wholeness in love. Such as coming home to someone or to something, irreversibly.

When this someone is taken in a storm, as they sometimes are — as they always have been — there is a narrow opportunity to recognize home in the ruins of that loss; to somehow find wholeness, even there. Because True Love is *not* taken in storms, and hearts break only when they are full of Love.

I am of the fortunate ones who have been broken open, not broken to pieces. How I wish that the enormity of this statement could penetrate and disarm your fears and doubts and frozen places.

We all have a secret wish we hope will come true before we die. For some it involves pushpins on a map, or digits in a bank account, or a Pulitzer Prize.

My wish has already been granted.

It is not a Hollywood myth, nor a literary fiction. It surpasses any words strung together in a Shakespearean sonnet, Sufic poem, or devotional chant. It exceeds all of that, beyond our wildest expectations, our greatest imaginings, the most masterfully crafted love story. My wish for you, Dear Reader, and, indeed, for everyone, is that we each have the privilege of experiencing, as fact, True Love, in its many forms.

It is quite probable that I was out of my mind when I wrote this. It is indisputable that this was written from a broken-open heart. In order to consecrate with me the sweet water harvested from my descent into the underworld's *cenote*, you must soften your gaze and read between the lines. You must open your heart and quiet your mind. You must be willing to feel the unspeakable.

I call to the wounded one.

I am here.

I will hold you.

I will ask you sharp questions and listen closely to every word and to every pause, and to every sigh.

I will let you dance, and stomp, and even break dishes.

I will feed you and rub your feet with oils.

I will call for visitors when you need noise, and turn off the porch light when you need quiet.

I will listen to your dreams, and write them down as if they were important clues to a fascinating riddle of resilience and humanness.

I will take you out dancing when the embers of your root chakra spark, and let you sleep in when you're tired.

I will spend all day and night with you, my precious, broken, hurting soul.

I will stay up late with you, thumbing books, and writing drivel, and circling the house two hundred times.

I will laugh when your madness is funny, and I will respond with confidence, intelligence and insight when it scares you.

I will make you tea.

I will let you be.

I will rent you movies to lighten the mood, and walk with you to the edge when you border the veil.

I will carry your shawl, and wrap it around your shoulders when you call to the stars and they don't respond.

I will take you home, and tuck you in.

I will listen to you, Wounded One.

I will never cringe at the graphic details of your war tales, or at the darkness of your humor.

I will believe in your ability to survive this descent, always, and without doubt.

I will trust every dip and zenith of your voice, your mood, your cycles.

I will never leave you small and shaking, Wounded One.

I will never doubt your power, your courage, your competence... even when you are a puddle on the floor, even when all you want is to die, even when you believe in nothing, care about nothing, think you are left with nothing.

You will have *me*, Wounded One.

I am wisdom and grace and a vessel infused with the purest love.

I have walked a thousand lifetimes, and I am here again.

I told you then, and I tell you again,

I am here.

I will never leave you.

Come home to me, Wounded One.

I am here.

THE LINES WILL DEFINE

I will return to India.

On the banks of the river Ganges,

I will kneel in the sand, soft and thin.

I may or may not notice the speckles of gold that we once admired glinting on the shore…

My destiny or doom will be written all over my face, and the lines will be the ones to decide.

I will listen to the water rush by,

and I will either curse Mother Ganga,
or I will praise her,

for I am sure your voice can be heard in her currents,

and the shape my face has taken by then will determine whether that sound will be sweet or haunting.

I will return, perhaps as a Crone, with years of smiles etched in my face, remembering you with gentle gratitude.

Or maybe I will go back an unrecognizable hag, cursing the place that forever darkened my spirit… with wrinkles that show that only tears have carved my cheeks and my every day.

The lines on the map will show if each crossroad was met with wisdom or foolishness, with grace or profanity, with resilience or defeat.

They will mark the places where I either expanded or contracted to this wild love and loss, where I hosted courage or cowardice or callousness in my belly.

In any case, I will return to the holy site,

where your life ended,

where our life ended.

I will kneel in the sand, in the same way I did when I midwifed your soul into the next realm, somehow knowing how to guide you towards that blessed and wretched split in the clouds that opened the gates for you, but not for me.

I will return to the place where our dreams washed up like driftwood, lifeless and empty.

To the river Ganges I will return, perhaps to take a dip, or to take my life, or to take my grown children to meet the joy and horror of my past.

I will return to India, even if only in spirit, as my body grows cold from a stray bullet or an illness or old age.

I will soar across the ocean and kiss the sand where I last touched your feet, and beg Mother Ganga, once again, to take me to where you are.

I will peer at the sky for the parting of the clouds where I last saw you, and follow your scent.

I will return to India.

I can't explain the visit from the Eagle, or the song you sang to me over the fire the night before you left. I couldn't try to lay my interpretations on the dreams, before or after the accident. Or on the words you spoke to the wise man.

I can't explain why or how I paused to breathe you in one last time before boarding the rafts.

Or the bandage you wrapped around my bruised rib hours before you left me.

…When I held your feet while praying over your body on the river bank, my heart was literally wrapped in a bandage that you had dressed me in.

Not the strange sensation I had when I woke up in the tent with you on the morning of the accident. A steady, warm, golden light being poured into my core. Like God herself was doing reiki on me to prepare me for the worst day of my life.

How could I call it less than magic?

How could I name it anything other than grace?

How could I pretend to dismiss or rationalize the last words you spoke, from inside the whirlpool, recounted by Natalie in a voice that may never cease to tremble, "Keep Swimming…"?

I cannot take credit for the stranger-than-fiction anecdotes and antidotes that someone and something sprinkled onto this pill that no one should have to swallow. Like sugar on sour candy.

That somehow make the unbearable, survivable.

They are simply colloquial, folkloric, true, divine.

How can I not bow in humility to whatever spirit moved me to give my deepest thanks to you in the dinner circle on the eve of your death?

Who am I to make "sense" of the mystery?

I wouldn't dare.

For the ways we are held by grace even as we fall from grace, I can only give my deepest thanks.

POBRECITOS

The first conscious memory I have of falling in love with you was on the night of my ninth birthday. After the party was over, and I had brushed my teeth and put on my Care Bears nightgown, I sat on the hardwood floor by my bed and laid out all of my new toys in a neat little row. I picked up the stuffed animal that you had given me; it was a white bunny rabbit, with pastel-colored polka dots on its ears and bow tie. I took it to bed with me, and hid it under the covers when my mom came to kiss me goodnight; I didn't want to have to answer any questions as to why I had chosen that particular new toy to sleep with. To my relief no one ever asked, but I never forgot, and I took that bunny with me, instead of the others, when we packed our suitcases and returned to the States months later.

You would bite your lower lip and shake your head at my corniness when I would tell that story at dinner parties, but underneath your cool little show, you were glowing.

You had loved me ever since we were children, also, even though you would only admit the cutesie truth to me, alone, while we washed the dishes after our guests had gone home.

"So, I see you're embarrassed by our corny little love story?" I would prod, turning my body away from you only slightly, waiting for you to take the bait...

"*Pobrecitos!* They can't imagine what we have, and don't know what they're missing," you would tease, hooking your arm around my waist, pulling me towards you with a soapy hand, my pouting mouth twisting with flirtation, refusing to keep up my tantrum.

"Why rub our fairytale in their faces?" you would whisper, the shape of the words on your lips tracing my cheek.

"*Pobrecitos...*"

I am one of those strange creatures who have been to the other side.
My spirit embracing yours as it hovered over your body.
My body refusing to obey and release me.
Trapped in this flesh cage, my broken heart keeps beating.

I walk in between.

My spirit united with yours, in the blessed eternity to which we
promised ourselves.
The place from which we come, the substance of which we are
made, dusts my hair, as if it were I who had been buried.
I am drenched in elsewhere, yet I walk in this world.
A place I once inhabited and now visit, as if for the first time.
There is such a thing as hell on earth, My Love.
I know this now, as you and I have known heaven, in this very place.
I wake to my own terror each morning.
Unraveling in this tug of war between defiance and obedience, I
bitterly write this, instead of a suicide note.
Because, even in this tormented rage and in this incredulous
rebellion, I am humbled by those sacred medicine moments
when the electricity of the source, Herself, pulsed through us and
spoke to us.
It was in these divine glimpses that we irreversibly understood
our place.
We understood, at least, that we do not understand.
That we should not — indeed, would never — impose our unknow-
ing hands into the realm of deciding who lives and who dies.

And so I dare not go with you.

It is not within my jurisdiction to make that choice; it is not
my right.

Every cell in my body aches to leave, but I stay.
I stay, soft and surrendered, waiting for the promised honey to flow through my shattered edges, to make me whole again, or for the merciful shards to slice the thread which holds me here.
I wish for death.
I beg for mercy, and I am here.
This is not a choice; it is not resilience or resolve.
It is neither nobility nor wisdom.
It is not even reverence for life, or loyalty to the living.
I am here, but just barely.
More ghost than woman.
Reduced to a minuscule ember, slowly suffocating beneath sedimentary ash.
Breathing the shallow, resigned breaths of a wounded creature, cursed and yet granted blood, flowing through her veins.
I lay here, helpless,
Watching the vultures circle above me,
waiting for life and death to settle their battle.

PHOENIX

To tell the whole story, go back, way back,
to the fringes of your memory,
to the places you cannot remember and cannot predict.
Try to find, somewhere in your bones, traces of the first meteor
shower, the first volcano erupting…
You *are* made of lava and the cosmos.
You *are* a tiny speck of stardust.
You *are* a particle of the whole.
Every cell is a compass.
Surrender and surf yourself whole again.
Breathe yourself back into the flow.

As the dust settles, you must remember something old.
Older than these broken bones, older than these bruised ribs and
bleeding lungs.
This story began long before the tsunami, and still it continues
afterward.
It's a story we all begin and end alone.
Think back to *before*.
Before your soul was merged with his.
Before two paths melded.
Before you found your place on the planet.
Your refuge, your oasis, your rock.
Your home, your most sacred, precious, perfect home, in him.

Look back further, Little One, to coral, granite, canyons and flame.
To the place where we all come from, this unnamable source,
older than time, infinite, perfect, Divine…
You will find yourself through the old stories; they echo both
forward and back.
They encode a map home.
You were born with it.

It is with you now, at this very moment.
It can be resuscitated, through remembering all that has come before and all that your soul is yet to endure.
The future will gain weight and texture.
And so will you.
Your cheek touching the gravel on the road, and the sage-breathed breeze.
Vast skies and velvet-winged birds awakening your sleepy, homesick chest, to sing over the bones of this ghost that you are, to watch her grow flesh and breath and a spark in her eye.

Dig up the one who is here now, who has always been here.
She who's had lightning love and thunder loss.
The one with walking boots and a hand drum.
The one who's danced with magic, and had a love affair with grace.
Her mane has known a few tornados, and her teeth are sharp beneath the lips she has polished soft for kissing and wooing and treasuring and adoring.
Underneath this tragic, veiled, Juliet-widow, lives a wild one, with strong thighs and notches on her belt.
She is made of fossils and bulbs,
Neptune and Mars.
She knows the whole story, one that began before the womb and will continue on, far after the tomb.
She tells the story with mountain chalk on the cave wall,
with a steak knife in the bark of the oak tree,
with a spray can under the bridge.
She tells the story with a melody she hums, when no words will do.
She will tell you a bigger story than the one you know.
Go back and find her.
She lives, then and in the future.
She is waiting for you.

I WRITE

I write for the broken ones,
the hurting ones,
the ones who hold the hurting to their chests,
the ones whose knees are blistered from picking pieces up off
the floor.

I write for humanity, glorious, pathetic, profane,
cellophane and gravel,
eternal and fleeting,
the living and the dead.

I write for the aching ones, the yearning, the fearful, the faithful.
I write to save my soul, to pull her back into my body,
for her to recognize herself, for her to speak.

I write for your soul; I will forever be reverent, faithful,
brimming with gratitude and honor for your soul, Mi Amor.

I write for *our* soul.
Our braided and soldered, intertwined, sacred unity.

I pray with you, My Love, the way I did with your hands in mine.
I plead, from this irrevocable oneness that we are,
for both of us, because you are my flesh and blood,
you are undisputedly inside of me, the seed of my wasted womb…

I write, for both of us,
the story we were blessed with,
cursed with,
the story that made us what we are,
one and broken,
simultaneously together and torn apart.

I write from my arteries,
tender, vulgar,
animal and divine.

I write for the dividedness of our very human nature,
for the pain and pleasure of a beating heart.

I write from the throbbing torture of being alive,
and the fog of half deadness.

I write, if for nothing else, to distract myself from the drumming
desire to die.
To vomit one pearl amidst the pus and the blood.
To remove the gravel from my throat, I write.

I write because silence is defeat.
I will not reemerge in the land of the living with my basket empty,
will not return from this wretched wasteland, this dark descent
without a blood transfusion
from the mother womb,
without pomegranates and gifts,
for and from the One who has called me down,
down,
down into the depths of human anguish
and grace
and resiliency.
I write and I study and I listen carefully,
so as not to let it all be in vain,
so as to drain the futility from this derailed train,
so as to give our story honor.

I write and I wail and I pray, My Love,
because this writing desk is my cocoon,
and I must melt,

must dissolve,
must mourn who I was,
who I longed to be,
in order to take on what I have been invited to become:

A healer,
a midwife between the worlds,
a medial being.

I write because if I do not choose to accept,
I will languish, as will the hieroglyphs of these scars,
senseless and sore, their hidden meaning never discovered.

I allow myself to write every little piece that comes,
no matter how abstract, or crude, or untalented, or incorrect.
I simply tell the story, as if to an old friend who has finally come
for tea,
nine months after my life was blown to pieces.

And as I tell her the story, she chimes in
and reminds me of the glimpses of grace that have somehow
infiltrated the darkest of rooms,
and I suddenly realize that she was here all along,
as I ran — as if set afire — towards vanishing witch-water,
begging for relief.
Finally I see that she is here,
listening to my story, and helping me to tell it.
She has been here all along.

I cannot see the form, cannot draw the map.
She surprises me at every turn, doing with me what she wills.
I only know that when I sit at the writing bench, something
will come.

Something speaks through me and for me, and I scribble away,
perking up my ears to catch every word and pause she dictates.

I write for someone I have not yet met,
someone hanging from the precipice by a strand of spider web,
with the hope that my words and pain and healing may be a
harness.
Perhaps for baby Jeremiah's granddaughter, many years and
miles from now,
or for Clarissa, on this very day, somewhere nearby, being beckoned
by the call of the rapids.

Mostly I write for myself,
because she who knows the way will only take the lead when I
let go.

Tiny, disposable, ceramic cups, filled with chai, warm our hands. We are leaning on our elbows on the giant stone steps that look out onto the river. The morning air is thick with humidity and the smell of spice and cow dung and human sweat and burning bodies. There are flies and lovely music and pilgrims who have finally come to bathe in the sacred river, at this auspicious ghat. There are goats and children and candles, incense and rotting piles of garbage. There are very, very old men and women, hunched on their canes, scanning the river for the death they have been waiting for. As Hindus, they believe that they can be spared reincarnation if they are lucky enough to die in Mother Ganga's embrace.

"¡Qué locos, estos Hindúes!" you whisper to me in your raspy coyote voice, between short sips of spicy chai, your gaze never leaving the river. "It's sad to think how much suffering these people have experienced, to want to escape from this life and the next one. Life has been good to me, Sarola. I love my life, and if I were given the chance to do it all over again, I would, in a heartbeat."

Days later, it is I who scan the horizon for a death that will not come for me. It is I who make offerings to Ganga and to all her sisters and brothers, asking that I may be spared another round, spared a new life, spared *this* life that has become so heavy and full of suffering that I wish for nothing more than to be released from this body.

"Tell me whose life you would prefer," my dad asks, as I stare blankly at him from across the table. "Who has been so blessed, with such richness and texture and intensity of human experience? Who would you rather be? Think about all of them, those you imagine have been dealt better cards. Those who have it easy.

Perhaps they are not hurting with this intensity, we cannot truly know. But tell me, who has loved with such intensity? Risked and lived and surrendered with such faith? Would you rather have never known him, never loved him?"

Of course not.

I would do it all over again, in a heartbeat.

PRISTINE

Haunt me sweetly, My Love.

Visit me gently.

Help me to keep what is clean, pristine.

Help me to make what is timeless, immortal.

Help me so that...

When I think of you, I think of the magic you made while you were alive.

I refuse to let your life be shadowed by the cloak of Death.

I refuse to let your very existence be defined by its having ended.

I refuse to let your name take on the stigma and stuffiness that the living hold around the dead.

When I think of you, I will not let my mind wander to hearses and autopsies and obituaries, nor will I let my heart wander to the sharp and steep sinking of abandonment and obliteration.

Our story together ended with you splashing me playfully from the other raft.

The curtains closed there, and our relationship here on this planet, in these bodies, ended.

Help me to mark the close of that chapter.

Otherwise, I will not be left with the sweetness of our love affair in my mouth when I conjure up your face in my memory.

If I am not careful to close our story with us laughing on the rafts, then your sweet image in my mind could easily be plagued by those of a lifeless body lying on the beach, a bleeding sheet on a stretcher, a coffin being lowered into the ground.

Those images are not part of *our* story.

They are part of my story.

The story that came after.

The horrific nightmare that began the day I found your body on the beach, the day the air from my lungs would not bring you back to me.

You were not there, on that beach, with your feet in my hands breaking my heart.

You would never break my heart.

You were no longer in that tender body, which I once knew as well as my own, when we circled around and thanked you, and blessed you on your journey.

Our lives together had already ended.

Those events will not contaminate the precious love story we had.

No, My Love, you did not hurt me, did not leave me; our story was not one of heartbreak.

It was beautiful.

It was joyful.

It was magical and healing.

It was after you exited this realm that my heart was torn to pieces.

You passed through the gates of death… but you are not death.

You are not darkness, are not pain, are not a tombstone.

All of that is the aftermath, the compost; it's what I am left to deal with Here and Now, in this new life that began the day we ended.

When I think of you, I will protect the floodgates of my memory from the stench of rotting flesh. I will keep your image clean, vibrant and soft. I will remember you as you were…

In love with me, blood pulsing through your veins, sweetness and spice on your breath. Endless kisses on your bubblegum mouth, for me and only me.

When I think of you, I will think of my childhood friend playing with me in *la plaza* where we grew up. I will think of us dizzy with beer and music and dancing and lust at Recorcholis.

I will think of you standing at the gate of my grandparents' home, calling for me with chocolates in your pocket.

I will think of body surfing at sunrise in Mazunte, and cooking lemon crepes for breakfast in Guatemala.

I will think of you heating the rocks for *Las Lobas'* temescal, and of how my body moved when you played the drums.

I will remember eating Top Ramen with cheese on rainy days, and reading books to each other under a blanket.

I will remember the hundreds of teenage nights in the shadows of the overgrown sidewalks of Marcos Paz, the longing of our bodies pressed between the trees, the cry of the owls above, and the song of the roosters announcing it was time to get home.

I will think of the love letters and long-distance phone calls, and I will remember the bliss of baggage claim, the heat and relief that came with spotting you in the crowd.

I will remember reading each others' minds on long car rides, and the way that wrestling could always settle an argument.

I will think of tearing down walls and building bridges, of burning sage at the feet of the redwoods.

I will think of long walks, of dinner parties and spicy shrimp.

I will allow myself the visceral memory of butterflies in my belly every time we made a move. I will remember holding your hand while boarding planes and smacking your ass while you carried all the heavy moving boxes.

I will remember painting the kitchen green, and moonlit gardening on the roof.

I will think of our stupid inside jokes, that eventually became a dialect of our own.

I will remember the way it felt to be known and seen.

I will remember being forgiven, and forgiving.

I will remember the way your voice sounded when you said my name, and the warm smell of your skin on our sheets.

When I think of you, My Love, I will think of our life together...

Of how astonishingly alive we were.

Haunt me sweetly my love.

Visit me gently.

Help me to keep what is clean, pristine.

YOU KNEW

You always knew that I was for you.

I was sweet sixteen the first time you told me.

The summer was ending, the night was over, the sun was visible in the sky when my grandmother came out in her slippers to kick you off her porch.

I was boarding a plane back to California in hours, and I had a no-good boyfriend waiting for me on the other side.

Brother and his guitar had sung us through the night, and you wrote in a note that you snuck into my journal that you felt like there was an elephant on your chest.

My grandmother watched me walk you to the gate, and in that good-bye hug of "childhood friends" you whispered in my ear that you were in love with me.

Since that day you never stopped saying it.

Through all the years I wasted on that no-good boyfriend, and all the summers you could have me, but only for the summer, and then all the years I didn't come back…

You loved me.

And I loved you, like an unwrapped gift I carried in my pocket. A little seed that could blossom in time, a "maybe someday" that often made me smile to myself.

That is, until my travels made me extreme, so far out on the fringe that I couldn't remember my roots, or the home I had known holding your hand on the benches of *la placita de Marcos Paz.*

I rang the doorbell at my Tiá Cecilia's house, unannounced, with torn pants and broken sandals that still had tar stuck to them from the long Brazilian highways I had hitchhiked to get there.

At first sight, my family didn't recognize me.

But you did.

You showed up at the gate, hours after I had arrived.
Like you always did.
How did you always know where to find me, My Love?
You were shaking when we hugged, though I pretended not
to notice.
Tucumán was no longer home.
I did not fit into its cookie-cutter shape, with my radical ideas,
my long dreadlocks and my muddy feet.
Nothing was as it had been, except for you.
You were still my friend, and you were still in love with me…
after all those years.
You told me so, of course, as you always did.
With that perfect blend of confidence and vulnerability in your
voice, which always penetrated my armor, and won the battle.

"Oh no, Harry…" I would protest and challenge… "*Yo soy loba,
soy loca, soy salvaje; nunca me podrás domar…*" "You'll never be able
to tame a wild, crazy wolf like me!" You could not be discouraged,
your sure hand reaching for mine as I spoke. "*Cambié mucho. Ya no
me conocés…*" "I'm different now. You don't know me anymore."

"*Sos la misma, Chiquita. Sucia, con piojos y plumas, pero la
misma que siempre amé. Sos para mí.*" "You're the same, Little Girl.
Disguised with feathers and dirt and lice, but still the same one I
always loved. You're the one for me."

You always knew.

RIVER

While traveling with our students in India, we were hosted and greeted by many locals. The introduction rounds were often painful, each side of the circle jerking awkwardly in its own way, not sure whether to offer a handshake, a hug, a *Namaste*.

It often went something like this,
    "Miru nam Olivia."
    "Ohleevjah?"
    "Yes, and Ethan."
    "Eeytun?"
    "Yes, and Andrew."
    "Undroo?"
    "No, Andrew."
    "Aanndoo?"
    "Yah, sort of…"
Until it came my turn…
    "Miro nam Sarita he."
    "Oh! Sarita!" they exclaimed, overjoyed to be able to pronounce my name! "Sarita Ji!"
They smiled and laughed.
    "Sarita is good Indian name," they gabbed, heads bobbing.
    "What does Sarita mean in Hindi?" I asked, every time, just to make conversation.
    "River. Sarita is river."

As my dear student Daisy would say, in her silly sarcastic tone, after stepping in cow dung, or missing a bus because *it* came too early, "Cute, India."

Real cute…

In the nightmare, my brother was crushed by an orange Indian semi while crossing the street. I woke up in a panic, not because I thought something had actually happened to him, but because it was a reminder of a truth that seemed to loom over us, the painful awareness that accompanied our every picnic in the sun. One that few choose to acknowledge, but all must eventually befriend... We are fragile creatures, with intricate, perfect, butterfly-wing-frail bodies that house these souls.

We knew that our bond would not be broken by human hands. That neither he nor I would ever walk away from this gift. And yet, some part of us was preparing to be parted. We called it a sequel to my mother's death. We called it, as Martin Prechtel does, "the hint of grief which is in all praise." We called it irrational fear.

Whatever it was, we were well aware that we were not guaranteed each other, unlike most of our peers who — like us — were healthy and young, and had no good reason to wake in the night with cold sweats, trembling at the fear of losing each other. Our mortality was exposed on the surface.

In order to soothe its sting, we toasted to our love at nearly every meal and prayed together most every night. We wished on stars and eyelashes and dandelions and *capicúas*.

We spent thousands of nights lying together in what we called *octopus position*, every limb coiling each other, reveling in the treasured late hours that replenished us after a long day, our lips morphing between kisses and whispers and prayers. "*Thank you, Great Spirit, for such a gift. Somos los más afortunados del mundo,* We are the most fortunate people alive. *Sos mi tesoro,* You are my treasure. Grant us the grace to love and care for one another honorably. Help us to be big enough to gently hold each other's broken places with patience and compassion. To successfully feed and call forth each other's gifts. Allow us to have and hold and shelter each other for the rest of our lives."

We fell asleep, clinging to each other so tightly you would think a tornado was coming. We woke up entangled and relieved.

Now I wake up alone. Now, my worst nightmares have come alive. I do not have my best friend, my family, my confidant and guide to help me through this excruciating pain. I have lost the only one who could walk me through hell in one piece. The one person with whom I could mourn and heal from a loss of this magnitude. The one person who could leave a hole so huge.

The night we were awakened by my nightmare in Bodhgaya was terrifying and tender. Sleepless and sacred. Grasping at each other's flesh while making sacred vows that it was not with these fragile, biodegradable bodies that we were in love.

"This is not you," we whispered, while clawing at each other's chests. "This, which I can lose. This, which can be taken. This flesh is not what I am in love with," we wept. "Our love is eternal. Our spirits do not die. Our love will outlast these bodies. Our love is never ending."

"I wish we all had an expiration date stamped on the bottom of our left foot!" I wailed. "I can't bear not knowing how long I have you for!" He laughed at me, in the soothing way he often did that took the weight of the world off my shoulders.

"Of course we can't have an expiration date, *Loca!*" he teased. "We wouldn't be able to live one day the way we're supposed to, if we knew what day it will end."

I had one month left with the love of my life, the night we had that conversation.

It has been years since I have been able to cry without Harry holding me. It was only in the safety of the home we built around each other that I could soften and fall apart. I am learning to cry alone again. I call on the memory of that night in Bodhgaya with rancid nostalgia, reconstructing the sensations of his mouth on my forehead; my cheek on his chest; his arms, my armor; his soft voice, hushing my cries. It's as if we were granted, on that hot night in northern India, a moment out of Time's order, waves of the future rippling into the present. We were given the chance to mourn together what today I mourn alone.

I was too panicked that night to pray, my bottomless wailing surprising him and me both. It was his prayers that finally soothed me back into stillness. It was the lullaby of his earnest and humble voice, asking for courage to surrender in the face of such danger; for Spirit to have mercy on our fragile dreams; for us to find peace in this dance on thin ice. It was his gentle whispers that finally rocked me back to sleep, as the window's light turned from violet to pink, the night stars hazy and vanishing.

I can hear him still…

WISE MEN

We were not the type of folks who got into Gurus.

We were far too slow to trust, and too skeptical.

But when the group itinerary led us to sit in on one of Mooji's *Sanghas* in Rishikesh, we left surprisingly impressed.

His teaching, simple and grounded in love; his temperament, humble and funny.

We resonated with him.

We returned with the group a couple of times to listen to his stories, and each time left with a sensation in our bellies of having touched truth.

The group was invited by our sponsor to have a private talk with Mooji. We would be welcome to ask questions, as is practiced in *Sangha*. Neither Harry nor I planned to ask a question. We liked the guy, but we weren't interested in being anyone's followers, and figured we'd let the students have the time with him.

During the session, I was flooded with a question, which, when I said it out loud, I realized was more like a statement: "I hear a lot of emphasis on 'detachment' and 'going within' and 'finding the sacred there,' and I'm curious about that, because I find that my most sacred experiences of the divine are actually through loving actively. I find God, by loving God in the other."

Just then, Harry jumped in, "Since we're on the topic of love…" he grinned, his eyes shooting between Mooji and me, "I am deeply in love with this woman…"

"Oh!" Mooji chimes in playfully. "Did you know that?" He looks to me, the whole room bursting with laughter. I nod my head girlishly, squirming on my cushion at the feet of the Guru, locking eyes with my beloved.

"So, I love this woman," Harry continues, "and I'm terrified by the thought of losing her. I would eventually recover, if she went off with some other guy, but, if she left her body... I couldn't handle it. And I hear about un-attachment, but I just wouldn't trade one ounce of this love I have for her, to get rid of this fear. It is worth it."

I didn't hear much of Mooji's response. I was too busy making googly eyes. What I do remember him saying, to both of us, is that our love for each other should not be a weight and should never limit the other's experience; that our fear of losing each other should not pressure the other not to live life fully.

One week later, we were being called to load up onto the rafts to enter the rapids. We stopped to embrace, and paused a little too long for my comfort. I was afraid. I didn't want to do it. Actually, I didn't want him to do it. I was afraid of losing him.

I can't explain how it is that Spirit can be so gracious and cruel at once, but, in that embrace, I placed my cheek on his sun-kissed skin and thought to notice how sweet and soft and warm and heavenly it was. I breathed him in at that moment, with awareness that it was not forever, that it could even be the last time...

That 'hint of grief that is in all praise' was palpable in that embrace. I considered asking him that we not do it, but these rapids were not supposed to be dangerous; they were supposed to be fun. "This is just the same, irrational fear that I feel every time he leaves the house," I reassured myself. "I cannot let it paralyze us." I remembered Mooji's words and forced myself to let him live. We entered the rapids.

Later that day, I am on a mattress of the floor of the orphanage, wailing at Mooji's feet. The students are all circled around with a horrified glaze over their eyes, watching me. He had been called to see us, apparently; in my insane ranting I kept naming him.

Of all the places Mooji could have been on that evening, he was at the ashram next door. After listening to my cries and my prayers and my questions, and praying his own prayers with his giant hands cradling mine, he spoke to me and to the students, for a long while, most of which I don't remember. "Its funny," he said, with that unshakable softness in his face, as if anything could be funny. "I was just talking with a man at the ashram next door when I got the call. This young man had died and been brought back. He was trying to describe to me how beautiful death is, but couldn't find the words."

I remember Paulo speaking in a whisper at my bedside later that night, shaking his bowed head as I thrashed around on the floor. "I know. This is so, so crazy, *Niña*, and these people around here are all crazy, too." He smiled softly into the terror of my eyes, without flinching. "You've got this extreme Buddhist monk in the next room, discouraging your cries, calling them unhealthy attachment. And then this Mooji clown goes on to say things are funny. There's nothing funny about this, and there's nothing to do but cry, *Niña*. You can just cry."

Paulo was an older Brazilian man who had lived at the orphanage for many years. He was the papa bear, playful and unassuming. All the kids called him Daddy. He even had an honorary Daddy coffee mug. There was an ongoing game, played by everyone who shared the communal kitchen, to sneak to use Daddy's mug, mostly for the fun of being chased around by Papa Bear seeking revenge. It was like a game of Capture the Flag that never ended. Paulo had made a notable impression on Harry. With all the flowy, trippy, hippy energies floating around, they had found a sort of brotherhood in each other, talking *fútbol* and goofing off. I had teased Harry about having a man-crush on Paulo, and he admitted to it, proudly. "That's the most solid dude around."

What we did not know at the time was that Paulo's wife had died in childbirth when they were young, leaving him to raise two kids on his own. He had come to the orphanage when his grown children left him with an empty nest and with so much love still to give.

It is no coincidence that Paulo was the first to arrive at the hospital, just as they were wheeling my love away. That he was the one to carry me to the car. That he was the one to give up his room, so that I could be comfortable. That he was the only one to get me to eat anything that first day, an offering too magical and meaningful to turn away, hand-feeding me a *Kinder Bueno* — an imported chocolate love in our shared South-American homeland, a stashed-away treasure, Harry's favorite, my favorite, the special treat he would often bring me home as a surprise.

Paulo was my guardian angel, handpicked and guided by Harry, himself. There is no doubt in my mind. He sat beside my bed, day and night, with a ready hand to place on my forehead when the silence was broken by fits of belligerent wailing and moaning.

Until my own Daddy could make his way across the ocean to rescue me, he was the most solid dude around.

Impossibly, my cell phone rings in my pack as we break down our camp in the foothills of the Himalayas.

"I can't believe I can hear your voice while staring at these majestic snowcovered giants, Daddy," I say to him, excitedly, when I hear his voice on the other end of the magical device in my hands. His tone is contrived, and he tells me that his mother, my Memom, is in the hospital after having had an episode which may have been a mild stroke.

I ask for the number and call her hospital room. Miraculously, the call goes through, and I get to hear her voice. Harry, who has had one steady hand on my waist and the other on my shoulder since the call came through, takes the phone and sends his love and kisses to his Memom, our Memom. She was the last person he ever spoke to on the telephone. My tough-as-nails, eighty-three-year-old Italian grandmother from Philadelphia had teased the worry out of his voice.

"Don't worry, I'm not going to die here."

"You'd better not, Memom! We need you!," his laughter traveling through the static of the call.

Later that morning, Harry climbed the mountain with the support vehicle to the next camp, and I hiked with the group. I was quiet on the seven-hour hike. I saw and picked many giant, bright flowers along the way, but they reminded me of funerals, and I left them in little bouquets on the edge of the path, little offerings that resembled *descansos*.

When we arrived at the exquisite little lake at the plateau of our climb, Harry was nearly ecstatic, telling us all the story of the eagle. My love was not "New Age," was not haunted by shaman dreams, was not a disciple to any guru or creed or practice, other than to his beloved soccer teams. He was practical and simple and fair. And so, his enthusiasm about the animal totem that had visited him entertained me. I chuckled to myself that India could make a mystic even of him.

As the story goes, he had been walking the rim of the tiny lake, admiring the reflection of the snowy mountain in the perfectly still water, the crispness of the colors and the air, and an eagle circling above. He stopped and stayed perfectly still, admiring its flight, and then, to his great surprise, the eagle swooped down and perched its majestic body on a branch nearly too thin to hold its weight, at arm's length from where he stood frozen. Awestruck to get such a close view of the animal that had transfixed him when it was soaring above, he studied the intricate patterns on the animal's wings, and then, as he held his breath to prolong the moment, the eagle turned its head, and stared directly into my love's eyes. They stayed locked in a gaze, which he described as familiar, for what felt like an eternity, before the beast took flight to the snowy peaks again.

The next morning, at sunrise, we walked the circumference of the lake in meditative quiet, for nearly fifteen minutes. Suddenly, I stopped to peer out at the lake and broke the silence.

"*¿Dónde fue, Mi Amor…que te visitó el águila?*" He shook his head incredulously, with a huge grin on his face.

"*Sos brujita, ¿no?* It was right there, where you are standing, in that very spot!" He walked a few feet towards the water, to a flimsy branch. "Here. This is where the eagle stopped to stare into my soul. How did you know!?" He smiled like a superstitious child.

"I didn't." I shook my head. I didn't know anything.

I hooked my arm in his and continued our walk with the slow, familiar pace of grandparents who have no need to fill the silence, but whose conversation never runs dry.

"I had a very strange dream last night." I hesitated, then continued, his raised eyebrows urging me forward. "It was beautiful, but so strange, Baby. We were with Memom, sitting on the couch at a party. Suddenly, the two of you got up to go somewhere. I was not invited. No words were spoken, just an understanding that I couldn't go with you. So I stayed, sitting alone on the couch in the noise of the party. Moments later, someone or something came to me to inform me that you had gone to show Memom the gates of heaven. In that moment, I was afraid, but then I felt a deep peace, deep love, and even happiness. And there was liquid, golden light, pouring over me, in waves. It was beautiful."

We paused from the crawling pace our walk had taken to look at each other, and he wrapped his arms around me, recognizing the twinge in my worried face. He held me close to his chest, and sighed.

"Well, Weirda. That's a weird dream. But, that's all it is… just a dream." He kissed my cheek and we continued to walk the lake.

In those first, hellish days on the mattress on the floor in Rishikesh, I howled everything into the phone, my voice blaring on speakerphones in Tucumán and Alameda. I said everything but that, because I could not bear to tell the story which would lead me to ask the question I thought I already knew the answer to. I was convinced that Memom, too, had left her body since our phone call days before.

It was not until I had already landed in Tucumán for the funeral, that I dared to tell my father of the dream, and to ask if his mother was still alive. To my great relief, I learned that Memom was well, and recovering rapidly. Months later, I sat in silence on her plush couch, her rice paper hand in mine, for hours. Finally, I dared to speak, and the words that came out were those of this story.

"Ah yes," she closed her eyes, rocking slightly in her seat, as if to transport herself to another time or dimension. "I know that golden light. It's like hot oil that pours over you in waves. I felt that once, when they placed your newborn father in my arms for the first time. That golden light is God's ointment."

Hoy me detuve en tu mirada que raja el velo del dolor
y supe que hay algo más que percibir
en este mundo que todo lo muele y desgarra.
Perdido por perdido ya ves da lo mismo vivo o muerto
pero tu alma es otra cosa, tu alma es la que te mueve
tu alma es mi razón, tu alma es la fuerza.
El águila muerte siempre vuelve y afina su aguda vista
hoy cualquiera puede morir sin saber cómo fue vivir
yo sólo espero sin dormirme en mis sueños
estar tan lejos de esta ignorancia.

Y es que sólo eso, sólo eso
despierta en mí el viento que todo empuja
sólo eso, sólo eso
que más puedo esperar, sólo eso.

Y mi mirada puede ver por la rejilla de tus ojos
para espiar tu corazón que se quedó con un pedazo de mi vida
al tiempo que yo brote de tu sangre.
Hoy que no hay tiempo que perder
que todo anda a reloj
que se destruye sin razón
y la vida muere en un discurso
y alguien se encarga de encerrarte
y otro prepara el fin del mundo
y tan lejana queda la esencia
que sólo el hecho de encontrarte para mí
le da sentido a mi vida.

Y es que sólo eso…

—La Renga

I refuse to listen to El Viento Que Todo Empuja on La Renga's album. Ever again. I want to forever hear it through your voice in my memory. The last song you ever sang to me, on our last night together sitting around a barely lit fire in the rain...

We had prepared medicine pouches to gift to each of our students in the closing ceremony. Three days before we were to board the plane home, on our last night of our Himalayan rafting trip, we were to close in council of appreciation and mirroring on the banks of the River Ganges.

Instead, a storm came, which sent the group scattering to their tents. You wanted to build the fire anyways. You said it had been too long since you had built a fire, and I sat with you under the storm, feeding embers with breath, and song.

The ancient Boulders, guarding the crack in the earth where Ganga carved her body, watched, unmoved.

They, crystallized mineral memory, lining the open veins of La Pachamama, did nothing.

We, despite the terror that constricted every artery and cell, encircled your body.

There was nothing else which could be done.

It was what needed be done.

We ripped off the bondage that paralyzed us and opened the shackles of our arms, to release you.

We spoke our gratitude.

We wished you peace.

We blessed your journey.

The earth below us rumbled, electric currents charging our knees in the sand with gratitude and praise, and the river cried.

But we spoke clearly.

We did what needed to be done.

No time for undecipherable wailing.

These prayers, too precious to be muffled with cries.

These words, too sacred to be folded and hunched.

This ritual, too potent to be diluted with tears.

It was the heat on my back that held me up.

It was the golden light of your being, lining my spine like a salve, like a pillar, like the truth…

The truth which we promised to remember.

The truth about our core, our divine essence, which does not die when the body does.

The truth that resonated in the cavernous chamber of my chest, your voice echoing each instruction from the inside out, words you spoke through me, words I spoke through you, a mysterious language, impossible to repeat.

Too sacred to repeat.

Words that bow in utter humility to the divine, in absolute astonishment of the grace which finds its way into the most jagged of edges, the hollowest of canyons.

And when we had finished midwifing you through the break in the clouds, and they came to lift your body from the sparkling sand onto the gurney, then came the howling,

That unmistakable animal cry of inconsolable grief and ecstatic praise, shaking the walls of the canyon, freezing the air and the birds and the breeze, with the suffocating stillness of desolation, obliteration, condemnation.

The Giants watched, unmoved, while the real world crumbled, and Ganga continued her journey towards the sea, carrying you with her.

Open veins, bleeding us empty.

Bleeding us clean.

I remember the first days as one would a nightmare, blurry and incoherent and timeless. I can see me clenched in a ball on the mattress on the floor. I am wailing and calling out loud, from the pit of my stomach, for hours and days, "God help me! God save me!" "Dios Mió por favor!" But God is nowhere.

Suddenly, my focus changes, and I can see that the room is filled with worn, dark women, with trays of food I will not eat. A white-haired one drops tinctures on my tongue, and a little boy fills the bathtub. Someone is holding my feet. Someone is opening the window to let the breeze in. Someone is placing fresh flowers from the market by the door.

An old story I was once told around a fire, lifetimes ago, infiltrates the room for a moment of lucidity, playing out in my mind. It goes like this:

The man's home and entire neighborhood is flooded. He climbs onto the roof and watches the water rapidly rising around him. "God will help me," he repeats to himself out loud in a mantra, clinging to the filling gutters with white knuckles. A neighbor calls to him from a canoe, where his family is bundled and dry. "Climb down and we will paddle to higher land!" the neighbor yells. "No, I'll stay here, I'm waiting for God to save me." An hour later, the fire department sweeps the neighborhood, throwing out life vests to anyone they can find in a tree or hanging from a water tower, but the man refuses. "Thank you, but God will save me." A helicopter finally appears, and lowers him a rope and a harness. The megaphone booms, "Come with us, you foolish man! You're going to die here!" But the man will not move, and he continues to chant, "God will save me. God will save me." And, so… he drowns.

For that half-waking moment, I see that God *is* in the room, Her many hands tending to me. I can see them encircling me and reaching their arms out to me. I can see that my eyes fill theirs with tears; that my words, though senseless and in a foreign tongue, are heard and understood. I can see that they are trying desperately to alleviate me.

I don't know them. I could not have planned for them, and would never have expected them to be here, oceans away from any family I have left. But they are. They are here. They are helping me. They are God's hands, holding me.

Golden rays of light can pierce even the darkest of rooms, if we allow someone to open the window just a crack.

Finally, I let myself drift off to sleep for the first time in days, as a stranger's hands rub my feet.

WE SING

The orphanage was full of visitors that day. Ramana's Garden, just up the gravel slope from the Ganges, was humming. A neighboring school's field trip to Ramana's had filled the air with laughter and shouting. A startling cry on the wind whipped up the ravine from the river bank. One of the boys from the Saraswati school had jumped off the children's favorite diving rock, but never resurfaced.

You and I ran down the slope full speed, until a fellow volunteer met us on the path, shaking her head… "He's gone. They can't find his body, but he's gone. The police are already there. They evacuated the beach. He was caught in an undercurrent. He is gone."

Chin to chest, we climbed back up the hill towards the orphanage, where we found a cluster of girls looking to us with red eyes. They were the butterfly girls, as I called them, just on the verge of womanhood, soon to be ready to leave the orphanage and start their own families. I had hoped to lead a small women's circle with them before our time living at Ramana's was up, but we were swamped, and just two days from our departure, so I had let the idea go.

"Are you girls okay?" I asked the stupid question. They all shook their heads furiously. "Do you have a rock stuck in your throats?"

"Yes, Sarita Ji, we all have rocks in our throats," said the oldest with a trembling voice. I led them to a rooftop that caught a glimpse of the Ganges.

"We women feel with our whole bodies and we feel for the whole world," I began, "and the way we keep all these feelings from eating us up, is sharing them in circle."

We said a prayer for the boy, for his mourning family, for all of us who were touched by his life and by his death. I asked each of them to speak her feelings and her prayers, and I taught them some of my favorite circle songs, meant to harmonize us and to lift up our prayers. They sang me songs I had heard at *Satsang* and some others that were unfamiliar. The circle had tripled in size by sunset; young girls and old women, alike, were called by our voices to the rooftop.

That night, I asked you to come out with me to dinner. I felt raw and overwhelmed, and I couldn't slurp down ladled lentils and rice with 300 children, as we did every night. On the way down the dirt path to the main road, we came across a woman who worked in the kitchen at the orphanage and with whom I had no language in common. She was tiny, and worn, and had always greeted me with a bright smile. That day, her face was stern and softened at the same time. We fell into each other's arms by surprise, and stayed there for a long moment, until a gust of wind lifted sand into our eyes. Your hand on my shoulder, as we walked away from that moment frozen in time, said it all. That hand on my shoulder told me you were tenderized, and proud. Proud of your woman, who spoke the language of women, who held a place for women, on rooftops and dusty paths.

At dinner, I dove into a monologue of questions and answers and unanswerable questions. You listened while I sifted through the sharp and softening edges, through the shock, the sadness, the contrast of our utter powerlessness and the quiet power of our simple circle. I spoke about the women's circles I had been holding for years, with young, modern women who wanted to touch back in with the old, sacred ways.

"All those full-moon rituals, with flowery language and burning copal, they were all just practice. They were only to create the tradition. The circles were always meant for days like today, when life and death and pain and love have broken us all open, and we need the circle to hold us."

Finally I looked up from my plate at you. I had been talking with teary eyes since we were given our table, and you had not said a word. Our plates of Tikka Masala were cold and untouched; your eyes, warm, and radiating an admiration and a respect of which I thought only my father was capable.

"You are going to do beautiful things with these gifts and with your generous heart, Sarola," you whispered across the table, reaching for my hand. "You already do. You are a gift."

Less than a week later, I find myself on a mattress on the floor of the orphanage. The Ganges has taken you, my precious Beloved, from me, and I have not moved from the bed in forty-six hours. People come in and out of the room. They try to make me sip something from a straw, and give me pills that I swallow without question. They bring me a phone that's been ringing, and I can hear my sister's voice, but my own wailing drowns her out. She later tells me that I could say nothing, and only sang her name again and again. They cannot get me to eat, and I am terrified to sleep, for fear of waking up and finding myself here again, for fear that the images of your empty body lying on the beach will haunt my dreams the way they flood my waking eyes. Over and over, I am tortured by the sequence. Over and over, I am giving you mouth-to-mouth, shaking your corpse, and the blood that foams up from your lungs is everywhere I look.

There is a quiet moment on the mattress. Ram Charan has been doing reiki on me, and I can see the room I'm lying in, perhaps for the first time.

The butterfly girls open the door.
They circle around me, in a quiet, single-file line.

They sit at my head, at my feet, all around me.
They look to each other, unsure, and then begin…to sing!
They are singing my circle songs.
The ones I have carried in my leather pouch from rainbow to rainbow to firepit to rooftop.

They sing me my songs, my medicine songs, my circle songs, and in their voices I can hear Rachell and Shirley, Yuko and Priscilla and Sole and Yolle; I can feel Lili and Maren and Jimena, and the hundreds of women with whom I have sat in circle. Those far-away sisters who are bleeding for me on this day, who are too far away to sing to me… who may not have had the courage or the insight or the audacity to do so, had they been kneeling at the mattress on which I'm dying.

These little girls are the only ones for thousands of miles who could know these songs; they are the keepers of the melodies, the voices I need most. They circle around me and sing me my songs.

For just one instant, I am not alone.

GRANTED

Mi Amorcito, you were granted a gentle time on the planet. You were able to preserve a soft innocence in your thirty-one years. You never had to experience devastation and misery, never had to share your home with a crater, were never left homeless.

For this, I am somehow grateful. I would never wish this kind of suffering on my best friend. I carry the burden of it being I who have to traverse hell, with the bizarre relief that you not have to do so. Love is funny that way.

My dad kneels by my mattress in the orphanage, as I thrash around, howling unanswerable questions. He has crossed the ocean to lift the remainder of his daughter over his shoulder, and to carry her to the burial of her fiancé. He has come to sign the papers and to acquire the stamps to send the body of his beloved son home in a box.

For a moment, I become still, too exhausted even to weep. My father begins to speak. He tells me of a day, many years ago, standing on the beach with you. You had traveled with me to California for the first time, to bridge the worlds and connect the pieces of the divided woman you had fallen in love with. My father and his new son-in-law were beginning the task of weaving the web that would make them family. The two of you stood staring at the ocean.

"What are your plans? Your projects? What is it that you want to do?" my dad asked the near-stranger who stood beside him, the man his daughter was madly in love with, a man whom he had once known as the young boy who lived next door, lifetimes earlier.

"I just want to be with Sarita for the rest of my life," you replied.

And that was all you said.

My father's voice breaks for the first time as he tells me the story. "Take peace in the fact that your love, my son, our brother, was granted his deepest wish. He was with you until the day he died."

Perhaps it was my wish that was granted after all, for a lover's most noble wish is that the other's wish be granted.

Love is funny that way.

Durga's giant eyes followed our every move, with curiosity and a trace of mischief. The twist at the corner of her smile indicated the beginning hints of the innocent naughtiness typical of a nine-year-old awakening to the existence of love and romance in the world.

Quickly, we developed a game. One that mostly appeased her desire for an inside joke with the two trip-leaders of the visiting student group. One that sometimes, though rarely, grew tiresome. Anytime Durga crossed paths with me, sometimes with only five minute's lapse between encounters, she would ask, with a cheeky grin,

"Sarita! Where is Nico?" And my answer, originally prompted by her, rehearsed and never-changing,

"He's in my heart."

She cornered us in the courtyard, on the stairs, in the dinner line and sometimes clutching a towel on the deck between the showers and the sleeping quarters. Each time, asking the same question, never getting old.

"Nico! Where is Sarita?" And he, playing along, every time, with as much enthusiasm as when the game had begun, weeks before,

"She's in my heart."

In the weeks during which we lived at the orphanage, Durga was the wide-eyed child we interacted with the most, and certainly the most frequently, but I doubt that much of any other exchange was made.

Always the same question, and always the same reply.

Three days after Paulo carried me to the orphanage from the hospital where I had watched my beloved's body being wheeled away, I emerged, at his insistence, from the small room with the small mattress where I had been burning, wrapped in a sheet like a corpse at the burning ghat.

Helping me to my feet, then to the door, the butterfly girls surrounded me, casts to my shattered limbs, tiny construction cranes transporting my wreckage across the landscape, each slim hand assisting me in my walk into fresh air. Ten steps was as far as we got, to a place where some tall grass grew. They sat around me, and I felt the earth beneath me for what felt like the first time in many lifetimes.

"Look at that," a kind passerby whispered, "Someone planted a flower garden here."

The butterfly girls giggled at the compliment, quickly checking to see if their expression of joy had offended me. My face, blank like chiseled stone, refused to move. All around the place where we sat, a rustling could be heard. The younger ones, with eggshell feet and fearful eyes, were poking their heads around corners and from behind walls to get a peek at the stone silhouette in the tall grass that they had once known to be a woman.

A cluster of children, passing unaware of my presence, chatted amongst themselves until noticing me, for the first time out of my room since I was carried back to the orphanage days earlier, sitting like a statue, or a flower, or both, in the field. All stood frozen, with averted eyes that could not bear not to peek, with mouths that dared not to speak.

All but Durga.

At seeing my face, as unrecognizable as it was, her mouth opened impulsively to ask me I already knew what. She had asked me a thousand times. But, just as she opened her mouth, a gulp of air got caught between her throat and her tongue, and her mouth remained open, as if the words she had almost begun to speak would not allow her to close her jaw. Her eyes, too, wide with shame of the unspeakable question she had almost spoken.

And the stoic statue face crumbled just long enough to muster the faintest smile, to put her at ease.

"Yes, Durga. He's in my heart."

PROMISE

I spent most of those first days in Tucumán at the tiny altar I had
built in the upstairs bedroom of your parents' house. One by one,
your people took their turns sitting with me. I was like a ghost,
staring at the candle's flame, as if it were a divination instrument,
listening for what to say. For each, I had a story. For each, I had
words about your peace, words of invincible love. I spoke to them
about the song you sang to me around the fire on our last night
together, and the split in the clouds. I told them of your last words,
the wise man, the eagle, the premonition dreams, the Hindu
meaning of the Ganga Goddess, and the undeniable grace that
had managed to weave its way around your departure. For each,
I had a gift from you. A little something we had picked up at the
market, thinking of them. It was my sacred duty to translate back
to them the goodbye I had been granted and they had not.

When Lucas finally came to sit with me, I had no words. He
had said next to nothing in the three days since I had come
home without you. I could think of nothing to say to your stoic
best-friend-since-kindergarten, the keeper of a secret language I
could never decipher, the brother you never had.

In silence, I gave him the Ganesh t-shirt you had bought for him,
and hung the prayer beads we had picked up at the market in
Rishikesh around his neck. I went into a pocket and fished out the
one-rupee coin that, without knowing why, I had been holding
onto for Lucas, and placed it in his open palm. You and I had
thought it was funny that, to signify ONE rupee, it had the image
of a hand giving a thumbs-up. Maybe I was supposed to give it to
him so he would think it was funny? Why *was* I giving him this
random coin?

When he saw it, his eyes widened and welled with the tears he had managed to hold back until then. "Did he tell you?" he broke the silence.

"Tell me what?"

"Why this coin? Why are you giving me this coin?"

"I don't know why. It's weird. I just felt I should give it to you."

Lucas had the coin made into a necklace and wears it on his neck to this day.

You had not told me, Love, what happened the last time you saw Lucas before leaving for India. How, after years of keeping your opinions to yourself about his infamous habits, you had finally laid into him, the way a brother sometimes must. You gave him a piece of your mind, and told him to get his act together. Life is too short to waste it away.

Lucas rubbed the coin between his fingers, wiping his tears and shaking his head in disbelief. "That day, the day he came to say good-bye, and ended up saying a lot more than that, after we had parted, he stopped halfway down the block and turned to me. He gave me a thumbs-up. It was a question. It was, like, 'Are you going to be okay, Man?' I gave him a thumbs-up back. That was my promise. I promised him I would be okay."

TICKING

It was the night before I left for India, to guide the first of two consecutive semesters. We would be parted for over three months, the longest time away from each other in nine years. The ceremony was raw and sacred and simple. You and I, kneeling at our altar, weaving three strands of string into a braid. "We, alone, are too small and petty to weave our souls together," we prayed out loud. "But with Spirit's blessing and strength and grace, winding in and out, between and around us, we can learn to love each other in a good way. We can rise to see each other with your eyes, Father, to hold each other with your arms, Great Mother. Help us to be kind and gentle and compassionate with one another. Help us to love wholly, to honor each other, to care for each other as you would. Please bless us. Please grant us a long, sweet life together, Spirit. We are so in love. We have found our home, within each other. Please protect us and allow us to come back together…" And, as we prayed, holding each other and the braid that symbolized our sacred union, fat tears fell into my medicine pouch, yours and mine both, staining the hide with salt. Salt I sometimes search for with my parched tongue, to no avail.

Kneeling next to your body on the banks of the river, I pulled my Swiss army knife from its carabiner and cut the braid from your wrist. I tied it to my own, where it still remains, next to the one you made for me. Now, I can't tell them apart.

I cut the macramé band from your ankle, turquoise and brown stripes… it looks like a river. You had made it eight years earlier, after I taught you to weave, and you had been wearing it ever since. You were buried with an eight-year-old tan line where it had been.

But no one saw that tan line, except me. The casket arrived from India, closed, and remained closed. As we stood around it, dumbfounded, in Tucumán, I pulled the anklet from my pocket and pressed it into your mother's hand. I did this because I feared her stoic features and calm voice might never allow her to say goodbye. I did it because I feared she might never believe that it was your body in that casket, and when I did, she crumbled in my arms. For a moment, I stood, strong enough to hold her up and soft enough to let her fall.

I did not take the watch from your wrist. I hated that watch in that moment. And I hate it now. I hated it because it kept ticking, and your heart did not. Because the world kept spinning. Because the birds kept singing, as if it weren't the end of the world. But the officials returned it to me, after I had watched your body being wheeled away at the hospital. Those bastards brought it back to me, from your cold body, and it had the nerve to keep ticking, happily, because it was waterproof.

I want to smash that stupid fucking watch, the one we found in the free box, the one you were wearing the moment you died. It's at the bottom of the box of things I hate or fear and cannot touch, still marking the passing time, ticking away almost a year later, on its face showing India time. I hate that fucking watch.

I open a fold in my wallet that has been hiding from me all this time.
I pull out his handwritten love letter, a strip of lined paper ripped from a notebook.

"A donde vos vayas, mi corazón va con vos. Te amaré hasta el día que me muera, y después también… tuyo para siempre, Harry"

"Wherever you go, my heart goes with you. I will love you until the day I die, and afterwards also… Yours forever, Harry"

My knees buckle and I fall to the ground, wailing…
Is this true? Oh my God! Is this true, or is this bullshit? Is your heart with me? Did your love for me outlast your body? Can I believe in this, take peace in this?

Someone had better fucking answer me! I shriek, shaking the walls of the small room.

Just then, something ordinary and magical happens…

A white dandelion floats through the window, which is open just a crack,
and it lands flat on my chest, directly on my heart.

And the burning tears turn sweet on my cheek.

Sweet like river water.

I would lie belly down on your grave all day,
if I thought it would bring me closer to you.
I would sleep with the smell of the sweet grass that has begun to
grow on the mound you lie under every night,
if I thought you were there.
If I believed that some ounce of you remains on this land, in
this land.
If I could convince myself that there in the box of bones I could
find you.
But you are not there,
any more than you are everywhere.
I cannot locate you on the map, My Love.
You are out of reach, as far as these mortal eyes can see.
I cannot take a bus or a boat or a train or a plane to the place
where you are now.
I can find no tunnel, no portal, no split in the clouds, no action to
be taken.
I would fight for you, was prepared to die for you, would never
have let you slip away.
I would have held your frail hand at your bedside until your very
last breath,
would have visited you every day in jail,
would have renounced everything,
followed you anywhere,
fought, till the day I died,
for you.
I would crawl across the continent,
swim across the ocean,
if I knew how to find you, Mi Amor.
I would happily leave this body, My Love,
if I believed that it would take me to you.

But I do not know how to travel to you.
I can see only a sliver of what there is to see,
and from this damned human perspective, there is nothing I
can do.
I am just a speck of stardust,
just a tiny ant, sniffing her way through an eternal mystery.

I have spent hours watching our videos, days swaddled in your
sleeping bag,
and months clawing at the mattress that was ours, calling for you.
I have smelt every tea cup and every t-shirt you ever touched,
but you are not there.
The only relic is my heart.
The only living, pulsing place I can find you is in my own chest,
between my own two lungs.
In the space that surrounds the hole you left.

I know that you would find me, would reach me, would rescue
me, Baby,
if you could.
"Hasta el fin del mundo,"
to the ends of the earth,
you promised to follow me,
and you did.
You promised to never, ever leave me.
You promised to love me for the rest of your life.
"Y después, también,"
and afterwards also…
And I believed you.
And I believe you love me now.
I believe you keep your promises,
although some promises are not ours to make.
What has split us surpasses our jurisdiction.
What took you from me was the only force capable of parting us.

This is the kind of distance that only Spirit can create,
that only Spirit can decide.
That only Spirit understands.

And we are left no choice but to trust Her.
To surrender to our own powerlessness.
Surrender to the fact that we cannot hold on to each other,
even though we vowed to do so for forever and ever.

I would lie belly down on your grave all day,
but you are not there,
any more than you are everywhere.

MANDALA MAPS

As the summer of 2011 turned to fall, Guadi and I spent nearly six months in a creative trance. We were inspired, enthralled — obsessed, even — with decoding the cyclical truth of all of nature. Days began with her whistling outside our window, under the flowering *Lantana* bush.

Every morning she called me from Harry's arms and onto the little couch that sat opposite our bed in the studio where he and I lived. Three rounds of whispered *mate* later, he would wake up, smiling and shaking his head at the mad look in our eyes, the scribbled diagrams on the floor, and the paint that splashed our wrists and elbows. We read and investigated and prayed and danced and painted and talked, late into the night, every night.

New moon, seed, darkness, winter-witch, stillness, emptiness
Crescent moon, sprout, spring, child, play, dream
Full moon, flowering, summer, mother, manifestation
Waning moon, harvest, autumn, crone dying, pruning, burning, descent...

We painted perfect *mandalas*, mapping our most fascinating find-ings, then designed and facilitated a month-long, living workshop called *Creatividad Cíclica*. Together, we hosted an experience for women seeking to tune into, and to honor, each moment of the inner and outer cycles of fertility, creativity, and the natural world, reclaiming the art of delighting in, and dancing with, the turning wheel, the macro and micro revolutions.

. . . .

Many moons and tears later she and I find ourselves in that very studio. I rip furiously at the maps and diagrams that had wall-papered nearly every inch of our home. Tacks and plaster flying, I strip every plan of action and mandala map from the colorful gallery that holds no future.

"*El futuro no existe!*" I howl. The future does not exist. I build a raging fire, a pile of papers and paintings and notebooks and dreams, twice the size of a body at the burning-ghat, which puffs smoke into *el cerro* for twenty-four hours from the rooftop patio that had been our star-watching tower.

Guadi and I stand squinting at the burning mountain of acrylic-smeared papers. She has agreed to the burning, but will not back down from her insistence on reminding me of its smoky contents.

"You *know* this map, Sarola. You *know* how the wheel turns. You know that it is not stagnant, that it will continue to transform. You know what comes next; it's all here, like instructions from the past, created for this very moment. You can't lose hope! You know how to open to her tides. You have been prepared for this."

Her pleas fall on deaf ears. None of it is useful.

"Empty theory," I hiss, the rasp of my throat as coarse as road burn. "What we could never have foreseen is that the maps are useless when we need them most. When engulfed in *true* winter, in the ancient ones' underground territory, you cannot see proof that the dawn even exists; you cannot imagine spring; you cannot be guided by these maps, because all there is — where I'm standing — is darkness."

The grandiose discoveries we made, lifetimes ago, in that one-room studio with a Lantana bush flowering at the gate…*pura ceniza.*

Pure ash

There is no preparing for this.

SCORN

"Where is your faith now, *Caminante*?" the strange voice hisses.
"It seems you are not as protected as you thought.
What made you believe that you were favored by the sun and
the moon?
Carried by the wind, embraced by *La Pacha* and all her children?
You are not special, are not immune to disgrace, not shielded
from tragedy.
Where are your guardian angels now, Little One?
The ones that made you so bold and so sure; they have
abandoned you...
Or, worse, maybe they never were.
Maybe they were a figment of your delusional mind, drunk with
your self-assured stories and testaments to magic.
It seems you are unable to walk, little *Caminante*.
Seems you can barely hold yourself up.
What now of serendipity and synchronicity?
What now, my little 'Warrior of the Light'?
Daughter of the Mother?
Child of the valleys and the rivers?
Your beloved Oxun took him from you, you silly brat, and you
are *desamparada*.
What praise can you give now, *Caminante* turned crawler?
I dare you!
I dare you to tell your pathetic story, you unlucky fool.
Tell us, *Caminante*.
Tell us of safety.
Of surrender.
Of how She's got the whole world in Her hands...
Tell us the story."

I am deep in a subterranean labyrinth. I can hear their muffled voices, calling down to me; they refer to a light I cannot see. They tell me to keep crawling, that I am moving in the right direction, and I force myself to believe them, even though I know that this is the blind leading the blind. They cannot see me, cannot reach me, cannot fathom where I am.

I call back to them, anyway, trying to describe the angles and the textures, the dead-ends and the sudden drops. Their voices are my only point of reference. Still, I know that I am the only one who can get me out of here. No one else can do the crawling for me.

There is no remedy, no recipe. The medicine comes in bite-sized doses, never the same, always changing. Silence and solitude, mosh-pits, movies, rituals and tea.

Without announcement, something sweeps through and straightens my spine so that wind and sound come full force from my lungs, and I am overtaken with an unquenchable thirst for wine and endless drum beats that will allow me to sing until my throat goes raw.

Suddenly it shifts, and I am curled up on the cold tile floor of the running shower, clawing at my breasts, and wailing.

Next, I am on a mission for a jean mini skirt and red lipstick. Nothing else will do.

Then three weeks of silence, lying on the desert floor, watching the circling vultures. Exposing this wound to the sky, as if to say, "Here it is, the blood and the gore, staring at your vast and nameless face. Do something! This is yours, too."

I follow each tunnel, clueless as to where it will lead me.

For a split second, my head pokes out from under the heavy soil that cages me, and I can see the labyrinth. I can see both where I have been, and where I'm going. I can see what has happened, and where I am.

In these snapshots, the lens varies in its effect.

In one flash, I see it all through rosy light. All is well in the grand scheme of things, and She's got the whole world in Her hands. For that moment, I take refuge in the belief that what is sacred prevails.

In another, the shadows are so stark and so long I can only see my life as a tragedy, and I am choked with self-pity and resignation.

Sometimes, I am a warrior-of-light in training, filled with purpose, my face painted, my powers to heal and to transform multiplying with every gate I pass.

At other times, numbness fogs the lens, and I am surprised by an indifferent shrug. Yes, this is the movie I'm playing a part in, but look around: everyone hurts; everyone loses. I am not special. This has been the truth about life from the beginning of time.

Often, it is shattered glass I am peering through. I just miss him, simply and viscerally, my body convulsing in abstinence.

All of these lenses, through which I see my reality in fleeting moments of lucidity, are true. Each holds its place, each is valid, each is entirely convincing in the moment.

And, simultaneously, none is entirely true. No reality stands alone.

Through these many lenses, I begin to build a shape of what has occurred, a relationship to its form. Slowly, I begin to wrap my mind around the absurdity of it all. With each snapshot, through each lens, I am constructing the story, piece by piece. A story I can live with. One that honors all of the facets of this descent. One that even welcomes and includes emergence and, the hardest of all, acceptance.

Most of the time, though, I am lost.
Disoriented by the dementia that has brought me to my knees.
Incapable of comprehending where I am.
Unable to conceive this inconceivable reality.

Mostly, I am enveloped with blackness.

Crawling and feeling.

Tanteando for tunnels that widen and climb.

I FOLLOW

She has her way with me, and I let her.
I let her in, a guest I did not invite, but must entertain.
I humor her and ask her what the fuck she wants of me.
This life is clearly not mine.
Not mine to own or design.
It was our sweat and blood, our dreams and prayers, that went
into the mud bricks with which we built our lives.
But there are only ruins where there was once a home, and we
have no one to whom to appeal.
It was never ours.
None of this is ours.
And, so, I stand here, bereft of everything I ever wanted, and
I rage.
What is it that you want?
Which is the life you will give me, now that you have ripped
away the one I built by hand?
How do you suggest I proceed?
But there is no recipe and no remedy, and, with the passing days,
my one-sided arguments with the elusive sky become subdued,
more earnest and sincere.
What is it that you want me to do?
I am here, and I still need you.

Grace me with your presence and your guidance, cruel and
benevolent Mother!
It is the least you can do!
I am yours.
I am left no choice but to follow you,
but,
please,
show me the way.

" *Si ya te he dado la vida, Llorona*
¿Qué más quieres? ¿Quieres más? "

~ *Chavela Vargas, la Llorona*

WHEELCHAIR

The alienation I feel in this absurdity of the day-to-day becomes unbearable, and I ponder a flight to Iraq to be with the victims of a war zone.

Perhaps people who are in daily contact with loss and despair could understand me; we could understand each other.

Perhaps I could find home with the widows and the orphans.

Perhaps the songs I am yearning to hear rise only from the ashes of palpable catastrophe.

Perhaps the potency of my song would resonate in those circles, would not be wasted on those circles.

Perhaps the chorus of an entire nation's wailing would humble my cries.

Perhaps their pain is much like my own, and they are much like me.

Perhaps this always has been so.

These daydreams wax and wane as the days pass in the second story of my dad's house.

From the bed to the bathtub, back to the bed… never going downstairs for more than a meal and a smoke.

And I bow in resignation to my own wheelchair and oxygen tank.

I am broken.

I am not going anywhere, for now.

For now, all I can do is pour tea for the blur of visitors peering at me from the other side of a veil they cannot see, from a state of oblivion that I do not understand and cannot touch.

All I can do is drop a fist-full of lavender salts into the bath and massage chamomile cream onto my cheeks, to keep the salt from my eyes from scarring my face.

All I can do is light a candle;
whisper a prayer, begging for mercy;
change the gauze, to try to stop the bleeding.

Iraq will have to wait, and so will I.

All I can do is wait.

RINGS OF A TREE

For eight long months, I watched the strange rings on my
fingernails move across my nail beds.
Tiny holes making the line, marking the time since my life
had ended.
Like Morse code, tiny holes that nearly reached my flesh.
The rings on my fingernails mystified doctors and shamans alike.
I did not need an explanation; I knew they were like rings of a
tree: a scar, a place where a fire or a massacre had been.
A place where it seems my nails stopped growing, for just a
minute, because I was dead.
Because my heart had stopped beating, and I could not breathe.
Because, for that instant, I left my body.
I looked down at it, kneeling next to yours, and it suddenly
felt absurd.
It was not mine. I no longer needed it, or wanted it, or even had
any respect for it.
It was meat and bones, lying next to meat and bones, and I no
longer lived there.
My place was with you, moving up and up towards the heat of
the sun.

It's still hard for me to feel my feet. The healers say that the soul
escapes up and out of the body when shock shakes the two apart.
I will need to do a lot of stomping, they say, to find my way back
in again, all the way to the ground.

Finally, I completed the long journey back to Tucumán, to the
place where we met as children, the place where we fell in love,
and eventually came back to make a home. The place from which
my most feared shadows had haunted me over the seven months
I'd been away, grieving you far from your grave.

I sat on your mom's bed after a silent meal and a jetlag shower, and finally snipped the remaining proof of my own death from the tips of my fingers, weeping silently. The scars are equally deep and raw, but now entirely invisible.

The rings had moved steadily and slowly forward, with every living, growing day, from the place of the present all the way to the past, and they became compost on my mother-in-law's bed.

I gathered the clippings I had been saving for this moment, to feed the soil of the olive tree we had planted in the backyard.

And then, I did something I could have never planned for, I painted my nails hot pink.

LOVERLESS

Without your fingertips to read my face like sacred texts in Braille,
I have become blind to myself.
I am a child at least, a sage at most, but not a woman.
These eyes spark for no one, and the cataracts begin to form.
These hips sway not at all, and the joints begin to fossilize.
I have no chase with creation.
I am fertile and fruitless.

The old rituals of painting my eyes with gypsy coal,
of smoothing my skin with sugar scrub,
of hanging beads from my neck and wrists, are lost.
And others are not…for there is a world of difference between
being in love and being a lover.
I still whisper, "*Buenas noches, Mi Amorcito*" to the crater in our
bed, every time I go to sleep.
I am an alien.

This idle body is calloused and uninhabited, dusty and abandoned.
As cold and hollow as your bones in that coffin.
My dreams sit stagnant, emerald pools in my eyelids, their nectar
a perished feast.
The wanderings and wonderings of my imagination, lost without
translation.
My mouth, tasteless and starving.
My mother tongue extinct.
I am in exile.

Frozen on the surface, with warm currents below,
I am an untapped reservoir of profound love,
love that's left the body,
mine *and* yours.
I will forever be in love with you, *Harrycito de mi alma*.

You are my love,
the love of my life,
but no longer my lover. *I* am loverless.

In seconds, this existence turned into a bad trip. A nightmare. A horror film. No one promised invincibility of the body. We knew the risks of living and of loving so intensely. The cruel surprise is in the torture of surviving. It is that this sort of wounding does not kill you. It hurts. It hurts like having molars pulled from your ribcage with pliers. Like razor-sliced lungs, like shattered bones, like slow torture that has you begging for death.

Despite every molecule in my body, which wants only to die, I am alive. Despite the hemorrhaging, my heart keeps beating. Despite its wretched brokenness and resistance, somehow, it continues beating.

I am haunted by this scene, playing over and over in my mind: *You and I, walking hurriedly through the rice field of a Nepali farm. In the heat of an argument about who knows what, you snapped back at my aggression with a statement so obviously true that it stopped me in my tracks: "I guess it's because all I care about is that you be happy!"*

No trace of sweet-talking or romance; simple truth. You lived to make me happy.

This is a responsibility I have inherited, a legacy you have left me. I dare not risk that you feel yourself to be a failure, watching helplessly from the other side.

Out of loyalty to You, Beloved, I try to soothe my own pain. In all my writhing and withering, a ceaseless whisper you left imprinted in my being begs me to be merciful, to suffer only as much as necessary, not to indulge in this torture. To seek light. To find relief. To care for your precious baby, who is hurting and needs help.

It began with the simplest of pleasures: *an instant of rest in a sunny window, where I could cradle a cup of tea in my shaking hands and taste honey. Yes, the worst has occurred; life is a living hell you cannot escape from; and…you are drinking a cup of tea, with a friend's fingers untangling your hair. This, too, is happening. You are with Rachell, and you can feel sunrays on your skin. The mint in the tea brings soprano tingles to your throat, while the honey adds its soothing baritone.*

I allowed myself every interlude that presented itself. It was the small caresses to my senses that soothed me most. The smell of flowers in a mason jar by my bed. The vibrancy of the silk rainbow scarves you bought me in Varanasi, draped over the window sill, banishing the grey from the room. The warmth of wonton soup filling my belly. The scent of cedar in the sweat lodge, which found its way into me even though my forehead never left my knees in all four rounds. It was with these small pleasures that I slowly learned to lure my soul back into my body.

These interludes grew, like any fragile thing that you feed consistently, making the spaces of rest between the waves of grief wider with time. The pain, when it hits, is as deep and as sharp as ever. The maturation that time has brought is my ability to coexist with the pain, to have a relationship with it, to know it.

I continue to move and to push, as I fight my way through and out of this hell. I fight for you, My Love. This is my way of honoring you. You only wanted to make me happy, and that you did. You made me so unbelievably happy.

Thank you.

I will take it from here, Mi Amor…I will carry on your legacy of love, so that you may rest in peace.

Of course I will fight, for you.

A THREAD

Through the Eyes of the Monarch

When Sarita was in seventh grade, *Titanic* came out in
the theaters.

It was months after her mom was finally taken by cancer, after
years of battle.

She had not cried at the funeral.

She had not cried enough.

And when she saw *Titanic* for the first time, she sobbed so
uncontrollably that the ushers came to quiet her down, because
there were complaints.

In the following weeks, a thread of wisdom within her tangled
twelve-year-old self led her to do something ridiculous and
brilliant.

She sought out an alternative to the therapy she was not offered,
and to the grief ritual into which she was not initiated.

She went to the theater, to see *Titanic*, sixteen times!

Each time, she cried all she could cry; each time, a little softer,
until it was only a few tears that trickled out of the corners of
her eyes.

I remember the day that she left the theater without having shed
one tear, and I knew It had served its purpose.

She was done.

JASMINE

I am Sara María,

Named after my grandmother, Sara Lía, although everyone called her Lolo.

My *Abuela Lolo* never heard herself called *Abuela*. She left her children young and motherless.

She never danced at their weddings, nor did she place wet towels on their foreheads as they birthed their babies.

My mother, Claudia, is now referred to as *Abuela Claudia*.

I imagine that she knew that she someday would be, as we hummed Amazing Grace around her deathbed.

I assume she knew that I, her eldest daughter, would soon begin to bleed.

Three weeks after we buried her, exactly.

I wonder if she knew then the shocking facts I learned in science class my sophomore year. About all my embryonic eggs being accounted for while I was still in her womb.

I wonder if Lolo was aware, as she carried my mother in her belly, hips swaying in the shade of a loose cotton summer dress, that I was inside of her, when my mom was.

And Jordyn was inside of my mom, even though she never saw Bethany reach eight years of age.

She carried Jordyn (at least a part of her) in her womb; she birthed Jeremiah, when she birthed Bethany.

I wonder if it ever occurred to my mom that there were none of her grandchildren peeking back at her from behind my eyes.

That I would be a young widow; that I would become an old maid.

I wonder if it ever crossed her mind, as she served dulce de leche cake on a flimsy paper plate to the boy from next door at my birthday party,

that his love for me would someday make me flower into a woman,

that losing him would make me wilt into a hag.

I wonder about the memory that we share, the hints of the future that waft into the present, like a strange scent on the breeze pouring in through the kitchen window.

¿Será, Mi Amor, que los hilos del tejido entre el pasado y el futuro a veces se estiran, se desarman, se entre-cruzan?

I marvel at the prophetic tunes of the past, taking shape and meaning long after the curtains close.

I watch baby Jordyn doing her ballerina dance, and I remember what Tía Isabel said about my own mother's dreams of becoming a ballerina.

She paints the picture for me:

My abuela Lolo's rich, church-choir voice, singing *La muerte del Cisne*, and my mother, her daughter, pirouetting in the dining room.

"*Siempre cantaba La muerte del Cisne*," she shakes her head, "until the day she went to give birth, and was given death, instead."

I think about the wedding we planned, Mi Amor; the theme, peacock feathers and abalone.

And the way the buddhists remind me to learn from the peacocks today…

It is the poison that they consume that allows them to create such extraordinary colors.

Be like the peacock, turn poison into beauty.

I am shaken by the off-handed remark from my Tia Isabel, on the way to the *zapatero*, as we passed the Jasmine bush that grows on the corner of your parents' house.

I had paused to breathe in the familiar sweet scent that came to be a symbol of our love.

The same bush we spent many nights pressed up against, intoxicated with its romantic scent and each other's breath.

"¿*Te gusta el jasmín*?" she asks

"*Me encanta*," tears welling up as I speak the words, saturated in the countless memories that coat my nostrils.

The potted Jasmine plants you gifted me on both continents, since I didn't like cut flowers, because they shrivel and brown.

"Don't give me something I have to watch die," I would order. "Give me something I can help grow."

"A tu mamá no le gustaba el olor del Jazmín Decía que olía a velorio… ¿Quién sabe por qué?"

And I can't help but agree with this stranger who gave birth to me. This woman I never knew as a woman. This woman who never had the chance to tell me about the irony of her mother's song or of the way the flowering Jasmines of Marcos Paz made her sad.

Indeed, Jasmine smells like funerals. I carry the weight of her prophetic memory as I plant in the plaza the Jasmine you gave me years ago, with your mother and sisters circled around. A burial of our own.

We planted it in the spot just between our two childhood homes.

Only feet away from the stump of the oak tree that my Abuela Lolo planted before she died.

EL ROBLE

El *Roble*, basically an honorary family member, grew with me.

It grew with the space between Lolo and the earth.

It marked the seasons that life continued, even without her.

It was the tree my mother would curl up against in storms, because her mother's soft lap had turned to bones.

The tree you would poke your head around when trying to catch a glimpse of me on the porch.

The one that hid us from the neighborhood when kissing goodnight.

The tree that called up tears my father thought had already been cried, when placing his hand on its living bark, years after losing my mom.

The tree that outlived Lolo, and Claudia, and Mónica.

The tree my grandfather was eventually forced to cut down, evoking wails that could be heard all the way to the *comisaría*.

The tree on whose stump you sat, under a flickering street lamp, holding me in your lap, whispering condolences as I cried for all that lives and dies.

For all that I have been blessed and cursed to outlive.

CHRYSALIS

Through the Eyes of the Monarch

Sarita now knows what I know about darkness.

About the dying of the self.

About spinning a cocoon and melting inside.

Literally, we caterpillars liquefy.

We do not simply grow wings; we turn into goo, and then reform.

I am watching over her, as I always do.

She is dismantled, taken apart; she is all holes and ooze.

No form, no memory, no consciousness, no hope.

She does not yet know what is to come.

She does not even know where she is or that she is.

Fortunately, her DNA does.

Her molecules are encoded with vital information.

They will be the ones to lead, to break her open and show her how to reemerge.

For now, from above, I see only a cocoon where my friend once was.

She is frozen in a tomb.

She never smiles anymore when I flutter by, does not remember me, doesn't even see me.

There is a frostbitten glass glazing her eyes.

Luckily, I, of all creatures, am not afraid of stillness, of darkness, of blindness.

I know plenty about tombs and cocoons.

I know what is to come, even though she does not.

I will not leave her side.

I will be waiting to welcome her back.

The evidence of you is fading.

Your imprint in me is so deep, so vast, so undeniable and irreversible.

How, then, can your fingerprints be so shallow?

How are they wiped away with the very turning of the earth, the passing of the days, the constancy of life taking place here and now?

Your old shoebox that we used for leather scraps and beads and feathers is fraying. I will use it for longer than is practical, and ignore the way it's been crushed and crumpled, and that the smaller beads sometimes slip through the cracks.

I will duct tape it, because I can't let your shoe box go.

It is proof that you were here, not long ago.

The day will come when every rolling paper in the house is most definitely mine, and when I find one in the bottom of a drawer, I won't rub it between my fingers the way I do, imagining that maybe *this* rolling paper slipped out from your wallet or out of your hands and into the box of colored pencils.

There will come a time when not one of the pens in the basket on my desk was ever touched by you, was ever used by your hand to write me a love note. The pens will dry up, and the lighters, too, and soon all the pennies I find, in every pocket and drawer, will be post-you.

Today I found a book we were reading together, *Cien Años de Soledad*. It had the bookmark from Afghanistan that you got in your Christmas stocking a few years back. I parted the pages where the embroidered fabric marked the spot where we left off, and I wondered if you had been the last to part those pages, if you had been the one to slip the colorful little strip of Afghan fabric between page 213 and 214.

Had I fallen asleep? Had I asked for more? Where were we lying the last time this book was opened? What had your voice sounded like when you read the last words on the page? Had I heard you? Was I daydreaming, or sleeping, or picking a fight, or seducing you as you read to me?

All I know is that I will never again open this book and wonder if your hands were the last hands to touch these pages. And another time-bubble bursts on the surface of now, and I wonder how many little capsules and treasures of you are left, in pockets and in old journals? How many hidden love notes can be left? If any. I hope for at least a grocery list in your handwriting. A coin that may have been in your backpack, a pretty stone that you mindlessly slipped into your pocket some afternoon on the beach.

Even if I leave the Afghan bookmark on page 214 for the rest of my life, and never get to the next chapter, I will never again touch this book wondering if you were the last to touch it. And, so, your fingerprints are wiped from the pots and pans, from my skin, which is changing and regenerating. I've cut my hair a few times now, since you've been gone, and I doubt that there's any hair left on my head that you ran through your fingers, that rested on your shoulder.

I know that, someday, I will curl up in a corner and continue reading *Cien Años de Soledad*. I will finish it, and I will cry for you. Maybe tomorrow, maybe in fifteen years. It is a little treat I am saving for myself, because maybe finishing the book we started together will somehow invoke you, and I will get to feel you closer, for just a minute, just one last time.

I can't bear to watch you fading from my home, and can't bring myself to slip my hand into the pocket of my winter coat, for fear that the last remnant of you is there.

Your fingerprints will someday cease to exist; every moldy grocery list will be in my handwriting, and every stick of gum will be mine.

Your imitation Aqua de Gio cologne from the Ashby flea market is leaking in a box, and I avoid it. The slightest waft of that smell tugs violently at my vocal chords, and out of my mouth come the strangest noises, like whale songs, like speaking in tongues, or whaling in tongues; and that is all fine, but I fear the day the smell will remind me of a box, and not of that heavenly spot above your collarbone where my face fit so perfectly, the engulfing warmth and waves of desire that my cheek on your neck provoked.

I don't want to smell Aqua de Gio ever again, and I sometimes have to hold my breath when sharing elevators with strangers. I want that smell preserved in memory, in you. I want the thought of that smell to take me to your neck and my cheek, resting on one another.

Then, there is the territory that must be reclaimed.

So I open the boxes with a volcano erupting in my chest and dust off the little treasures that were ours, but are also mine.

I speak to myself out loud as I pull each item from the box. I speak to myself in the soothing tone a mother uses with a frightened child, in the same tone that you often used with me and would most definitely have used with me today, as I do the unthinkable task of going through our things. Things that were ours and are still mine.

"This is your Aguayo blanket. You bought it in Guatemala, for your bedroom. It was both of ours, and it is still yours, and you can drape it over the pillows as you always have, even though this bed is cold and barren and far too big for you now. There, that's better; you needed some color in here."

"These are your boots, your favorite boots. They help you not to feel gloomy on rainy autumn days, remember? Yes, he bought them for you on a cobblestone street in Cuzco. Yes, you will see him every time you see them, and... These are your favorite boots. It's okay to wear them. That's what they are for. He loved to see you in these boots. You should wear them today, to cheer yourself up, because it's gloomy, and he bought them to help you fight off the autumn blues... He hated to see you sad. He would tell you to put on your boots today. You must put on your boots. C'mon, Baby, please put on your boots!"

Some fingerprints penetrate the skin.

BAPTISM

Ganga, Mother Alchemist,
She who washes, liberates, and sanctifies.
Delivering souls to the shore of the ancestors,
Ganga, holiest of rivers, only living Hindu goddess,
your waters blessed and praised,
by thousands of generations.
Holiest place in the oldest living city on the planet.

Some dare to say to me that you were beyond blessed to be taken
by Ganga Ji,
and Dr. Emoto's mandalas claim my eyelids as their canvas in
my sleep.

My hair has been streaked stardust silver, from calling out to you
from the branches of the highest trees, branches snapping and
bending beneath my weight, throwing me this way and that.
My outstretched arms reaching past the ozone layer,
over the Milky Way, I have traveled to the edges of the galaxy,
and much of my voice has become crumbly clay,
from breathing for you after your lungs failed us,
water and earth coating my ribcage.

My deep-water fish,
I cannot touch your velvety skin,
not even with the shadow of my fingertips.
I cannot live in your depths.
I can only hold my breath to dive so deep.

In dreams and in rituals kneeling at our altar,
You are here, with me…

But you are ever more stretched in reaching me,
and I am strained to hear you.

Months go by, and your voice is reduced to a whisper.
Sometimes, now, my cries for you are left to echo in silence.
I accept this symptom of returning to my body.
I give my soul permission to re-inhabit this realm,
because this is where I am now,
and anything different will become an illness.
I have seen the way the vacant ones' minds deteriorate when they
have traveled too far or too often to the other side.

I give you permission to go peacefully to where you now live.
We are forever intertwined.

And…

I allow the spaces between us to grow,
as you journey forward,
as I journey back to the world we once lived in together.

Because when I call to you, on the tips of my toes,
I sometimes fear losing my grip on earth and body.
I stretch as tall as I can, hearing your answer on the highest
winds, but I clench the earth with the soles of my feet,

Because I have seen living bodies, with traveled souls, absent and
unable to return.

Because I know I am in great danger, and people have lost their
minds with less reason than the ones I have.

I know I must wean myself off the Milky Way…

Last night, however, my thirsty pillow tasted one salty tear which escaped from the corner of my eye as I drifted to sleep. That simple gesture invoked you, after months of trying to leave you in peace, of trying to find some peace here and now. That silent, thoughtless prayer, that single tear that streaked my face, called you, and together we journeyed.

I dreamt you last night, felt the heat of your skin on my palms. It was you, undoubtedly. Those were your shoulders I gripped. It was the curve of your back I was riding on. You were my chariot, my guide, my raft.

Rushing me through the rapids towards the ocean.

I dreamt of you last night, the flavor of the lighting reminiscent of that year I dreamt of riding whales every night, gliding through the mysterious in-between place of the up-side world and the deep blue underworld.

You were steady and majestic, so familiar it seemed we had not been apart at all. My lucidity warned me not to fear the rushing water, the way I do when I am awake. And in the knowing that this was a precious visit, I was careful to study every freckle on your skin just one last time, my fingers memorizing the curves of your flesh, the texture of your skin.

I rode on your back through the rapids last night, My Love. I absorbed you, my cheek on your shoulder, my thighs wrapped around your waist. I was with you last night. I never saw your face, but I can taste you on my breath.

I followed you last night with the same surrender and faith as I did when I was eight years old, riding my bicycle behind you into the forbidden sugar cane fields in Marcos Paz. I felt the same exhilaration and absolute trust as when I was a lanky-legged little girl going on an adventure with her next-door neighbor. I felt the same, familiar confidence that - with you - I was safe.

I was always safe when you were there, and I believed with the instincts and ferocity of a lioness that, if I was with you, no harm could come to you, that my love was enough to right any wrong, to shield you from any danger.

I was wrong.

The stars crowded the sky last night as I rode on your back. The cool bubbling of the white and silver and turquoise sweetwater swished and swirled and sparkled all around us as we glided through effervescent jade and crystal caves.

In one dream, true sweetwater quenched the thirst of this desert year.

One salty tear called forth a river of sweetness in that moment out of time.

I was with you last night, and, now, I cannot look at the rushing water with contempt. There are traces of you there, and it may be your playful otter-spirit making the rainbow splashes on the shore.

Last night, this year of nothingness melted, and all was right in the world again.

I was home.

I was home in the currents, heading steadily to the sea that pulled you hungrily downstream.

Last night, for just that moment, engulfed in cool water and humming whale songs,

I was home,

back in the silver-lined place at the edge of the veil,

my ankles and elbows touching the underworld, my shoulders and face in the breeze.

I was a woman.

I was a mermaid.

I was a whale rider.

I was an animal.

I was with you.

I was one with you.

I was alive.

I was alive…

I was alive!!!

I wake to my own regret and desperation.

Nothing is right.

You are not here, and I am.

I am not a deep-water fish.

I am not velvety-skinned and ever shape-shifting.

I am here.

Trapped here.

Landlocked

and thirsty.

Harry and I were leading our first trip for Leap Now, a three-month adventure we ourselves had designed, beginning in our hometown of Tucumán, where the furthest remnants of the Inca Trail lie, and working our way up and along the ruins, overland, concluding our *peregrinaje* at Machu Picchu. We were halfway through the semester, volunteering in a wildlife sanctuary in the Bolivian jungle, just outside of Coroico. The monkeys were the most curious attraction.

All of the monkeys were said to be friendly and harmless. All but one. The alpha male, Sambo, was dangerous and, so, was kept tied up at all times. We were instructed never to look him in the eyes. I was sitting on the floor in a gazebo, with three baby monkeys either in my lap or perched on my shoulder. It was quiet and peaceful in the jungle. No one else was around, and for a moment I felt like Frida Khalo.

Sambo crept up from behind, ripped the baby monkeys out of my lap, and sat on my knees, staring directly into my face. He had somehow escaped. I was alone, afraid to move. I leaned back on the bamboo pillar of the gazebo and pretended to sleep, but he began to scream in my face. I tried to sing to him, but it only made him scream louder.

With long, dark fingers, he grabbed the bun in my hair and began yanking on it while he screamed, pulling my hair harder and harder. Then he bit me on my scalp. I did not yank away when he did. The monkeys' caretakers had explained that they bite and release, and, so, if a playful baby monkey were to take a nip at our finger, we should hold still.

Sambo had now climbed onto my shoulders, his long spider arms wrapped around my head. He bit me again on my forehead, all in a matter of seconds. Somehow, suddenly, I was on my feet, throwing him off of me. But it was too late. He had clamped his sharp teeth into my ear, close to the eardrum. My throwing him off of me with his jaw momentarily locked resulted in my ear being shredded. My head wounds were gushing blood everywhere, blinding me. I lifted my hand to my head and felt ribbons of flesh and cartilage where my ear had been. I looked at the crazed animal covered in my blood and assumed he had my ear in his mouth. I walked slowly away, down the path, past all the other monkeys, who were screeching and wailing, cheering or protesting... I couldn't tell which.

Following the long, winding path, down the hill and across the plank of wood that served as a bridge over the creek, and breathing steadily so as to not lose my balance, I arrived to where the group was working, cleaning cages. The flow of blood had drenched me to my hips. The women who worked in the kitchen were the first to spot me, and they shrieked frantically at the sight.

In a state of profound shock, I was totally calm... asking them all to step back, to bring me a chair, to find the phone we would need to call for a car. My students circled me, in hysterics. I had to ask a few of them, in my best leader voice, to go wash their hands, to refrain from touching me, to calm down, to find the veterinarian... but not to go find Harry.

My man was cool, calm, and collected, in 99% of the situations we found ourselves in, but I knew that seeing me this way would push him over the edge. He came running down the path, at just the same time as Ivanna, the in-house vet. He was panicked. The look on his face, at seeing me hurt and in danger, shattered me from the inside. At no point had I removed from the side of my head the bloody hand holding the remainder of my ear. They all fussed over the wounds on my face, but had not yet seen the real problem. Ivanna fumbled in her kit as Harry fumed and paced, fighting back tears, repeating over and over, "Who did this to you?"

"Take him over there and give him a glass of water!" I ordered. "I need to show Ivanna something."

He let himself be led away, or at least made us believe that he would, until the moment I revealed to Ivanna the mess of cartilage and flesh and skin that had been my ear. He brusquely freed his shoulders of the students' guiding hands and ran back, red in the face, to see what had happened to his baby. "My baby, my baby! I'm going to kill that fucking monkey!" he howled, and took off up the path, kicking gates and throwing things. It is the only time, in the nineteen years that I knew him, that I saw him like that.

They stopped him before he could take revenge on Sambo. Ivanna didn't dare touch the wound, more than to pour hydrogen peroxide on my head and to give me a balled-up volunteer shirt to stop the bleeding. The car came, and the three of us rode out of the canyon towards the nearest field clinic. The nurses there gasped when they saw what was left of my ear. "No. We can't do anything with that. We can't touch that!" They shook their heads emphatically and sent me to the Capital in an old jeep painted as an ambulance, an I.V. pumping antibiotics into a swollen green vein in my arm.

Three hours later, when we arrived at El Hospital Arcoiris in La Paz, they were ready for us. The surgery room was all set up, and within seconds they whisked me away on a gurney from poor Harry. I reached for his hand. The shock had worn off, and I was afraid. "If something happens in there and I don't come out," I gulped, "Find happiness, Baby. Find true love."

He never forgave me for saying those words, left to echo in his head for what he described as the worst three hours of his life. "I'll get you back, someday, for making me suffer in that waiting room!

. . . .

"Find true love?" he mocked, as we told the story to our students while digesting our lunch at the Ashish Café in Varanasi. We seldom told the story, because he claimed it hurt too much to remember. He hated to recall and to recount it. Let's admit it, though: it's too tempting a story to *never* tell it. So, whenever we did, he would try to joke about how dramatic I had been to say that.

But I had meant it. I had needed to say it, just in case. Just in case the instructions would be needed in his surviving me.

I lifted my hair, to reveal the scars, and showed off my plastic ear. By now, three years later, Sambo had transformed in the folktale into a gorilla, and the week I had been hospitalized in La Paz had turned into two.

"Find true love?" he bit his lip and shook his head. "She should have been a soap-opera star." He sighed, looking to the students for affirmation, but they were silent.

Raven's eyes were bloodshot with tears. "That's so beautiful," she choked, "You two are so beautiful."

I remember the first time I made it to the bathroom without anyone carrying me. Crawling breathless from my mattress on the floor to the toilet, pulling myself up with the towel rack, and, finding myself vertical, leaning against the sink.

I had not seen my own reflection since the accident, and the strangest assumption had become nearly fact in my mind. From my maddened state, I was convinced that, in the previous forty-eight hours, all of my hair had turned white.

Finally, leaning against the sink for support, I lifted my gaze to my own reflection.

To my shock, I found, there, in the glass, a picture of myself much as I had known her, my image nearly untouched, despite the feeling that I was mostly dead, that I had aged one hundred and eighty-three years.

Those who greeted me in the coming months often found my face to be changed, but never took note that I had become an old woman. To my frustration, my body continues to look like that of a twenty-nine-year old, and I have to explain repeatedly and with irritation that I am in fact two hundred years old.

In many traditions, when a woman's head of hair has turned fully white, she becomes empowered to touch every single member of the community, without taboo. In her crone-hood, she becomes universal in her place in the community; she becomes desexualized, and de-individualized; she becomes a grandmother of the tribe, to every woman, man, child, and elder.

To my disservice, my hair did not at all turn white, and I am quite the opposite of the grandmother of the tribe. I have become the dark witch in the cave that children tell stories about and adults avoid. The village has grown afraid of me, afraid of this sadness that fogs the mirrors and the windows, that paints pearls of cold sweat on the walls.

Cars that used to stop to greet me now drive by, waving uncomfortably. My brothers' faces have grown stoic, and my sisters' voices, shrill with oozing sympathy. I often find myself alone on the periphery of gatherings, despite the awkward attempts to include me. There is a hush that follows me into the room; there are those afraid to let me see their tears, and, worst, those who dare not laugh. Many are afraid of me. They are afraid of smelling death on me, or of saying the wrong thing. They are afraid of what I represent, of their own fear of tragedy percolating in my presence, of their own grief being dislodged from the safe sediment where it sleeps.

I am the face of death, "stigmatized and inauspicious," as Sanghamitra would say when explaining the social status of widows in India and the old tradition of Sati (where a widow is encouraged to throw herself onto her husband's burning pyre).

I represent our deepest fear, the worst of our nightmares.

During a Women's Circle in my dad's backyard, Maren voices what I can sense, but have not yet named. I have become *untouchable*. I am an icon of grief and catastrophe. "And yet," she adds with the impish grin of a wise woman-child, "in your healing and in your resilience you also hold the key to modeling our deepest hope. Your example restores our faith in unimaginable grace. You make us brave again."

There are times when the storm is too fierce and too sudden for us to seek refuge.

Times when all we can do is fall flat on our backs and hope that the violent wind and the acid rain will mistake our limp bodies, lying close to the ground, for a curve in the land.

When the leaves, ripped prematurely from the branches of the trees, are the only blanket laid upon us, the sap of their blood the only glue that tethers us to the earth.

There are times when gravity, alone, is not enough to keep us from flying away,

When it takes a certain kind of stillness and resignation to hold our place.

A stillness more passive than surrender.

A stillness much more like *being* dead than *playing* dead.

A stillness that does not dare to breathe, and that cannot muster a heartbeat.

For some storms insist on killing all that is alive, and the merciless wind will snap any bones that are still intact.

There are times when we have to become soft, soft like clay.

When we have to release the fists of our hands and let our palms lie open at our sides, as flexible as bamboo, bowing to a hurricane.

There are times when all things solid must dissipate, must dissolve.

When the rattling, throbbing hum of the torrential rain and of the roaring thunder must bury us alive.

And we can be grateful for that.

We can be grateful for hibernation and for resignation.

We can rest in nothingness, until the calm.

Until far after the calm.

Until whatever quiet aliveness left in us feels safe enough to travel up from where we lie among roots and twigs and worms.

An audacious tendril, poking out of the earth into the open space.

We can wait as long as it takes.

We must wait as long as it takes.

There are times when we must lie flat on our backs and be glad that we have been buried alive, even if we think we are dead.

Because, eventually, comes the calm, comes the dawn, comes the brave, green shoot which insists on orienting towards the light, towards life.

Comes that which never resigned.

This place that I have chosen is barren.
It's tough.
All stones, thorns, wind, and unforgiving sun.
I came here in a trance…
The idea of taming this little adobe home unexpectedly woke me
from my apathy.
Suddenly, I was rising from bed early, with a list of things to do
and acquire… mosquito net, machete, hammer, canned corn,
toilet paper, incense…
I stocked up the old vegetable crates I had been using as a dresser
in Tucuman
and made the move,
hardly thinking,
just trusting the impulse that had raised me from my bed.
Once the rent was paid, the pantry stocked, the light bulbs
changed, the cobwebs cleaned, I looked around… and panicked.
Why on earth did I choose this place, so desolate, so hard, so dry,
so lonely and isolated?
The green things growing on the land can be counted on my
fingers and toes,
and I have to account for each of them if they are to survive.
I have to move the old, leaky hose, barely dripping, from this
thorn bush to that *algarrobo*.
I carry the old paint bucket, full of water, from the shower faucet
to each patch of life,
and, by giving life, I am coming alive.
By hanging bright silk scarves from the windows and prayer flags
from the gate,
I am tilling the soil for my own revival.
This place demands that I put my bodily strength back into action.
The desert will eat this little house up, with me in it, if I become
too still.

She comes through the windows in gusts of sand.

The faucets grow clay, the insects take over.

The dirt floors need sweeping, the flies need swatting, the toads need puddles, and the veggies need chopping.

I cannot lie in bed all day, cannot wait for someone to put the kettle on the fire.

This place is not lush and fertile and easy, the way I like places to be.

Maybe, if my retreat were in the Caribbean, I would just keep lying on the beach, as I once lay in my bed, and the days would go by, and I would never wake up, never have to fight for my own survival.

It is the contrast of dry, hard-packed land that forces me to flower. Its starkness leaves me no choice but to be a force of balance.

This land is barely alive, and there is no room for a barely-alive custodian in a place like this.

I am moving, hammering nails into the walls, hanging watercolors, burning incense.

Cleaning out the old oven and filling the kitchen with the smell of coconut and dulce de leche.

This place is quiet, so quiet; my prayers are said out loud, with no one to hear them;

the wind is violent, and my broom's task is never done.

The days are long, and I am called to the writing desk between meals and chopping firewood.

I am forced to bleed into my pen, because without the sacred crimson markings on the page, there would be no color, only a sepia landscape, a dry valley,

a powder-blue sky, with few birds and no airplanes,

and no witnesses, no one to hear me cry.

My feet are getting tough again, my elbows and knees are scraped and bruised, and my muscles are reviving, after ten months of nothingness, of winter, of frozenness...

They are warming back up and into gear, carrying stones to mark

the walkway and lifting dirt into the new planter box, which was
once a tin can of kerosene.
They are moving the furniture around and around,
finding the right place for the old rocking chair,
and they are carrying me down the long, sinuous path to the market,
where I can pick up some *humitas* for dinner tonight.
Something wise in me rose and moved me to this parched place,
where I have to squint to see a tiny yellow flower on a cactus,
have to squint to see beauty and work to make beauty.
This place is a homeopathic remedy to my own crumbling.
This place is too lonely for me to toy with self-pity and spiraling.
My moves must be concise, and my feet must be planted.
I'm playing the music I dared not to play.
I'm filling the silence with stories,
tuning my ears to the distant birdsong.
I'm planting rosemary in an old tuna can.
I am taming Rontu, the wild and feared neighborhood dog.
I am greeting the neighborhood men with firm handshakes,
the women with sweetbread and tea.
Here I am, learning to breathe, with one wheezy lung.
Again shoulder deep in an uninvited initiation that will ask every
last cell in me to rise.
Alone again, howling for grace to find me.
Razor to skin, I sculpt a mohawk, instead of a tombstone.
Repeating in the mirror, "*¡Sos guerrera!* You are a warrior!"
Alone again,
learning to open cans with a steak knife,
spear tarantulas with an old broom,
and shrug at the noises the wind makes when it bullies thorny
branches against my windows.
I had to come to this hard and wild place,
which is mostly stones and thorns,
in order to call for myself,
to call to myself,
to hear the call…

I am walking with fast footsteps down one of the streets that borders the plaza on the way to the bakery, determined to go unnoticed. It's been many days since I've left my writing cave, but I have finally been forced into town for provisions. A neighbor greets me by name; I nod and continue walking, hoping not to get caught in the net of locals that surround him. A man, who is nearly entirely blind, looks up from his conversation at the sound of my name.

"Sara!" he calls out. "Are you Sarita, who lives on *la loma*?" It is midday, and he is drunk, with a pint of whiskey in his dirty hands. I have already guessed: it is Topo, the young widower I've been told about by well-meaning neighbors who don't know what to say when learning my story. His insistent invitations leave me no choice but to sit with him on the curb. The other men shake their heads and move over on the stoop, collecting tattered bills for the next bottle. "I know your situation. I've been wanting to talk with you…"

He slurs a speech, without letting me respond, for forty minutes, spewing advice, unaware that he is the very picture of what I fear for my future, and that I am taking his advice as exactly what I should *not* do. It has been twelve years since the love of his life died, and, there, on the stone stoop outside the liquor store, he cries, for her, tears that trickle down his face, but do not break his voice. I wonder if he is even aware that his cataract-deadened eyes are leaking for the woman he lost twelve years ago. Since her death in a kitchen fire, he has attempted suicide three times, all with fire.

"She told me to try to be happy," he whispers, the heat on his breath burning my nose hairs. "On the hospital bed, I was

Sacred heARTwork by: Sarita   **121**

kissing her. She was all burnt, and her lips were peeling off her face and sticking to my mouth. She told me that she was leaving, and I didn't believe her. I couldn't understand what that even meant, and she kept saying, "I'm leaving, but you have to find happiness."

He gives me a lot of advice, in one long, winding tangent that I can't always follow and am sure contradicts itself more than once. Finally, he admits that this advice is for himself as much as it is for me, that he is far from happy, and that he has not yet been able to do these things. And, so, I begin to listen more carefully.

Topo is speaking to me the deepest secrets of his pain, which he is sure I know as well as he does. He is also speaking of beauty and of love, with all the light and hope he can muster for a new initiate in a secret club to which he has decided we both belong. Even though we just met, even though I want no affiliation with him, or his club, and I can barely look him square on, for fear I might see myself.

He goes on and on, although I say nothing. He cannot see the tears streaming down my face. The old women selling tamales in the plaza can definitely see us. They are staring. We must be a strange sight: the broken, permanent fixture in the plaza and the quiet girl from *la loma* whom no one knows, crying together on the curb in broad daylight.

This stranger's words have opened the floodgates I have been needing, to cleanse my eyes, before the cataracts can set in. I just sit there, nodding, even though he can't see, because my vocal cords have been tied in a knot, unexpectedly, on the way to the bakery.

After a jolting, four-hour drive through the mountains from Marcos Paz, the old women put their bags down by the door. They have surprised me, but not themselves, by successfully climbing the winding dirt path from the end of the road to my splintered adobe home, stopping every few steps to filter the thin air of the high mountain through their tired lungs. They ignite the oven and pour gin and tonic as they begin to speak, at first conspiratorially, in a hush. Despite themselves, the giggling bubbles over and their volume skyrockets as they tell a bit more – and then even *more* – of the juicy details of love and affairs and death and the end… so many ends that were not the end, after all.

These women, who love you, Harrysito, as much as any pair of old women could, have come on a mission, unspoken and clear. They love you enough to come raise me from my sleep and announce between drinks – sometimes breaking into song to say it – that this end is not the end. They pull me from where I sit, heavy as iron in my dead-maiden's chair, with strong arms and rising enthusiasm. They pound the table with their fists in bouts of laughter and stamp their feet into the dirt floor. These women, cackling about the most ordinary and scandalous of *travesuras* — mischief long savored if perhaps rarely disclosed — while checking the *sfijas* in the little tin oven and prodding at the fire with an old broom stick.

These women are more than twice my age, their hair silver and blue and black, their eyes growing younger with each drink and with each turn of the stories… stories that put the *novelas* they watch each afternoon to shame. Stories that they weave together, together, finishing each other's sentences and revealing more than they had anticipated they would reveal, as my eyes widen with each revelation.

These women, sent to a lonesome shack in the desert, waltz in to tell me just how old I really am... not very old at all!

Life was shorter than I thought; life can be longer than I can imagine.

They have seen many ends that were not the end, after all.

Medicine people surround me.

Bowing in service to my initiation, carrying stories and bundles of herbs, their grandfathers' rituals and their aunties' sweat-lodge traditions, they flap flags and pound feathers on my chest. Earnest, hopeful, tracing the lines on my palms, seeking clues as to how to proceed.

Their hands on my neck and back, illustrating chakra pulses, humming, drumming, swaddling me as they themselves weep, for I am a pristine sculpture made from Kali's gnashing teeth. Chiseled by brutal blows, stone cold, petrified, and breathless. They tend to the embers, using their own long lives to rekindle this young, ancient, helpless, darkened spirit. They carry our picture on the Day Of The Dead parade, take our names to their prayer circles, bake brownies, send care packages, write letters, send videos and poetry and support for my writing. They speak to me through audio books and dreams, through Facebook posts and cardboard signs. They hurl ceramic plates on the kitchen floor, and dare me to do the same. They make mosaics out of broken mirrors, art out of broken dreams.

Medicine people surround me.

They are the dancing midwives of the Soul, who surf what is frozen, fluid. Who make what is broken, whole, in the endless rhythms of their waves.

They are the gap-toothed smile of the shoeshine boy; the long embrace where there was once a handshake; the one-line email that says it all; the ones who light candles and pour tea, speech-less; the ones who rent stupid movies, and paint my nails, and order pizza; the ones who guide me into the desert in search of a vision; the ones who carry their African tribes' grief rituals across the ocean on their backs; the ones who sing me the songs I once taught them, so that I will not forget.

Weathered and calloused grandfather hands cup this broken bird. "Aaah, so you're in hell?" they ask, casually, without prompting. "Welcome," they smile, "it will not last forever," and they hold me. They hold me, not as Great Spirit could, because only She could take this pain away. They hold me in solidarity. Powerless and knowing, at once. Yes, they have walked a thousand miles through hell, and, no, there is nothing that they or anyone else can do. Because as my teacher's teacher used to say, the only way out is through… There is nothing left to say or do. Nothing to do but surround me.

I bow to the medicine that surrounds me.

Her simple invitation allows me to dive to the sharpest places of my pain. I make no roadblocks, and I take my foot off the brakes. I surrender to the deepest, darkest, most visceral expression of my mourning. I reach a place where I can dig no more, cry no more, scream and shake and curse and beg and fight no more. Organically, the waves recede, and I crawl away, refreshingly exhausted.

Contrary to common belief, the pain is most toxic and dangerous when you dance around it. If you allow her in, and host her fully, she will transform, mutate and move through you. She will cook you to the point that your body can tolerate, and then pull you off the fire. She will not take you anywhere from which you can't return, if you look her in the face, and keep hold of her hand. She is a green-eyed monster of a teacher, and if you do not acknowledge her, do not make time and space for her, she will rot you from the inside, and nothing will move and nothing will change.

The Dagara tribe of Burkina Faso has a wise tradition of encouraging and witnessing the expression of grief, in community. My Dear Teacher and Soul Sister, Sobonfu Somé, has carried her tribal grief ritual to the parched soil of the West. She gives us permission to dive into the deepest expressions of our grief. We do so, not alone, behind closed doors, as is *our* custom, but instead with the compassionate strength of the village behind us, holding a drumbeat and chanting a lullaby that does not falter.

I can access my full range of love and joy and praise and reverence, only to the extent that I am willing to be with *this*, too. I can resurface, only as fully as I am willing to dive. And so, with Sobonfu's steadfast singing at my back, I press my cheek to the gravestone I have been dragging on my shoulders. It crumbles with the moisture of my unrestrained tears, and the load is lightened.

VANISH

It is said that man cannot divide what God has united.
I believe that even God herself could not, would not, divide what
She has united.
And so, my soul and yours are irrevocably one.
Some piece of me will always be connected to the heavens, and
not at home here.
Some piece of me always was.

Where your soul lives and in what form…
These are questions I am wise enough not to ask.
Wise enough to know that we who live in this material plane
cannot understand the vastness, the complexity, or the simplicity
of it all.

I *do* know that Energy does not cease to exist…
Never, under any circumstances, esoteric or scientific, does energy
cease to exist.
Energy transforms, or merges, or disperses, but it does not
vanish.

We are not from this place of flesh and bones and tsunamis.
We are made of stardust, of everything, of eternity.
My soul is united with yours, and *that* is unbreakable.
That does not vanish.

"¡Tengo miedo!" I called back to him, my eyebrows swallowing my eyes. He splashed me from the other raft, in that annoying, big-brother way.

"Never let go, Rose!" he called out, inviting the students to join him in trying to tease the fear out of me, and they all began to sing the *Titanic* theme song, "My heart will go on…"

"No, no," I hushed them, shaking my head. "Please, no sinking-ship music!" I demanded, forcing a smile.

I was looking back at him as we approached the rapids. His face was the last thing I saw before the white water.

His last words to me:

"Find true love!"

HOPE CHEST

I will not pack a chest of lost hope,
a box of treasures, collecting dust, taking up space and haunting
me from the back of the closet.
I will not keep you locked up in an airtight capsule isolated from
my breath.
Your mug from Oaxaca will not become a relic in the museum, a
keepsake, a discontinued dream.
I will drink coffee with cinnamon from its fragile belly until the
day it finally breaks in the sink.
Because that's what it's for.
Because that's why we wrapped it in newspapers and brought it
home with the tomatoes and squash that Saturday at the market.
Life did not end, as unfathomable as that is; it changed, forever.
I was sure I had died, sure that there was no tomorrow, sure that
I could not survive,
and yet I still drink coffee with cinnamon on some rainy afternoons, Baby,
and I will drink from your cup, because you are a part of this
moment.
I will make space for you.
Space for your picture in my wallet.
Space for your name in my voice,
for our stories at the dinner table,
for our plans in my maps.
Different…
deformed plans;
utterly obliterated, decimated,
vacant, useless, heartless, miserable, hellish, desperate,
changed-forever plans.

But this ship is still sailing, inconceivably,
broken mast and torn sail,

and I'm lost without our maps, which hold so many clues.
And hot coffee with cinnamon on rainy afternoons is sometimes
my only source of pleasure.

I will not put my medicine pouch away,
even though I hate it because it smells like your burial.
I need it now more than ever.
I will use the Tibetan incense burner that we bought for our
wedding ceremony in that back alley of Kathmandu,
even though it was only lit once…to send you off.
It is filled with the prayers of those who blessed you, and thanked
you, and mourned you, and celebrated you.
It is filled with our excitement for November 16th.
Our gratitude for each other, and the commitment we made, and
our desire to celebrate this love with our tribe.
I still celebrate the gift of your love with our tribe,
and I will light that shiny bronze incense burner on the full moon,
because you liked it, and you liked the full moon.

Those circle songs we sang around your lowering coffin
are the same ones you sang with me around the fire;
they will not be banished from my ears and throat.
Those melodies will kindle this flickering fire now.

I will cook your favorite dishes, because they're my favorite also.
I will laugh at the parts of the movie we thought were funny,
because they still make me laugh…unbelievably.
I will see my own reflection in the mirror with the tenderness of
your eyes and I will conjure up the memory of your sweet bed-
time prayers, allowing them to rock me into the same peaceful
sleep as always.
I will not negate you, neither your imprints nor the gaping hole
you left.
I will not hide all evidence of you;

I *am* evidence of you.
I *am* remnants of you.
I *am* because of you.
I will not put our things in a box, My Love,
will not lock the life we were living under a crystal case.
I will not make a monument to lost hope.
I will drink coffee with cinnamon,
and sing our songs around the fire.

MEETS THE SEA

"There is a breadth and a depth that comes from having weathered the most ferocious and furious of storms. There is a merging with the greatest mass, when we cross the threshold of this sort of initiation. There is a knowing that comes, as massive and vast as the oceans themselves. Never again can we cry over spilt milk, after having cried over spilt rafts in white water, spilt blood, and massacred dreams."

I leave these words open on the screen and ride my bike to the Boulder post office.

The man at the counter looks at my name on the manila envelope,

> "Sarita? Oh Sarita! Who gave you this good Indian name? Sarita is river, good name, such a very good name."

> I feign a smile and nod, "Yes, yes, I've heard."

> "And when will Sarita meet the sea?" he teases.

> "Oh… I don't know…" I try on my best head wiggle. "What happens when Sarita meets the sea?"

> "It is in our old stories, our mythology, would you say? That when Sarita meets the sea, she is married."

And so it was. I made my eternal vows to you, only to let you go. The ultimate test and sacrifice. The highest of prices to pay, for the most precious of treasures.

I was asked to give you back to the sea, like *Alfonsina, vestida de mar*. A part of me went with you.

133

Forced to release you, my wedding vows morphed into siren songs.

I watched my entire life flowing downstream, rushing to merge with Yemanja.

My dreams, my future, all that I was, all that I hoped for drowned with you.

The heart I gave to you has been claimed, swallowed, abducted by the vast, vast sea.

And now it is to her that I am wed. Great master of currents and the changing tides. Great mystery, her depths unknown to human eyes. Great Mother, womb of all of life. Open, endless, bottomless beast. I am wed to her.

" The ocean, she is vast. She was the first one here, and perhaps she'll be the last. "

~ Gemma Luna

PURGATORY

I am in limbo
no longer on the other side
but not yet here

My struggle has turned invisible

I seem to be okay
but I am not

I am trying
there is accountability and risk in that

I am flailing and failing
there is resentment and overwhelm and exhaustion in that

I am revving my engine
but this hill is steep and I can not find traction

I am tired, and though not as old as before, still very old

I am waiting

waiting for fireworks and champagne
waiting for a welcome-home banner
waiting for a finish line

But the small everyday struggles are private
they are quiet
they are slow and tedious
and have no witnesses

I am not finished,
as much as we all would like for it to be that simple

This is not a victory, as hard as I have fought,
as tired as I am of fighting

I am not back, just because I am no longer a ghost

I am not okay, just because I am no longer obliterated

I am not moving forward, just because my wheels are spinning

But I am not motionless,

not any more.

I am not want-less

and I am not resigned…

there is honor and hope in that.

Having a Death Wish was like being invincible. The stakes irrelevant, the playing-field infinite, and the veil more seductive than scary. The beauty of a Death Wish is having nothing to lose.

I begged for Death to take me, not because life without him is not worth living, but because of the kind of intolerable pain that calls for euthanasia, and the belief that the giant boot that had squashed most of me should be merciful enough to put me out of my misery.

My worst nightmares had become reality. My soul ripped out of my body when his did. All ties and investments in this realm severed, all bets off, all dangers belittled and darkly humorous, all fears vanquished. I could not conceive of another blow so brutal, could not fathom ever caring again.

The dust has settled now. Inconceivably, the nightmare has beauty beginning to stream through her thick eyelashes, and my heart is welling up with love again.

The irreverent heartbreak of a corpse-bride finally sets down her mask, revealing who is still here: an open-hearted woman, a human, vulnerable and powerless.

Vital force, returning to my body, slices me open, its blessings and burdens a double-edged sword. The wound which had begun to caramelize over, to coagulate and to close, begins to bleed with the realization that I still love so much, it hurts. That the world did not end, that I did not die, and, therefore, that I still have so much to lose.

Returning from the Ethers back to Earth means agreeing once

again to this dance on thin ice, with even more aching scars that map the dangers and the excruciating praise one must have for what is precious and what is fragile.

Loss is not something for which we grow calluses. Practice in the art of grieving does not make us immune. The fear only grows with every burial, every heartbreak, every disappointment.

I freeze in terror…when my dad's routine doctor's appointment takes just a little too long, when my baby sister drives the highway just a little too late, when one of my brothers forgets to return my call.

The post-traumatic mutations and mutilations begin to reveal themselves now:

As I weep for baby Jeremiah, and the likelihood that his beautiful, dark skin will close doors on his brilliant, bright face; that his sweetness could turn bitter; that his perfect baby mouth may someday hiss the uNspeakable Word that he heard on the radio; that some bigot might someday perceive his presence on the sidewalk as a threat, and gun him down, for wearing a hoodie, for being a black man, for crossing an invisible line.

As I spin little Jordyn in her tutu, my eyes welling with the possibility that her three-year-old ecstatic dancing may someday become twerking; that she may begin to dance for the attention of shallow men who call her a ho; or, worse yet, that she may someday simply stop dancing, because her future holds heartbreaks and disappointments and losses from which I cannot shield her.

I would lay my body on the track to stop the trains that could steam through and wreck her.

I would carry a grown Jeremiah in my arms to any corner store to which he ever needs to go, to avoid some bullet mistaking my boy for a man to be feared, for a thug, for a criminal.

I would break every bone in my body with my own hands and build a fortress of marrow to shelter them,

I would rip every one of my organs out to keep them alive,

I would spend my every waking moment kneeling in a pew, if my prayers could protect them.

I would change the whole fucking world, just to prevent the luster in their eyes growing dull.

I am tortured by longing for that which is still here, by worry for that which has not happened, by grasping for that which is not guaranteed.

With a terror of Tsunamis.

Eterna y vieja juventud, que me ha dejado acobardado. . .
Como un pájaro sin luz

~ *Homero Expósito*

The future has made an enemy of me.
She has made a mockery of our plans, and turned vibrant symbols and clues and hieroglyphs of hope on the walls into a smoking pile of trash. I have been betrayed and overridden and spat on by the future.
She is dead to me.

And yet, she has the audacity to court me.
That bitch!
Her white gloves twirling a parasol above her head.
Her serpent eyes daring me to meet her on the edge.
She demands that I come out and play,
although she promises me I will not win.
Demands that I make a decision,
which she will be so kind as to accept as a suggestion.

She is a dictator, humoring me with her questions, disingenuously soliciting my input.

She tosses me a pencil, while patting the eraser in her pocket.
It has been over a year since I've written a to-do list, since I've attempted to map a plan or a vision. I shake my head in defiance.

I have refused to engage with her.
She is not pleased.
This lady is a bully.

"If you do not come out to greet me…" she stomps one dainty boot into the ground with her arms crossed "…No future will ever come, and you will be left frozen in this hell. If you reject my invitation to dance, you will never again hear music. Believe me, you want me to exist."

BOMBS DROPPING

Everything is not going to be okay; not necessarily.
We know this, in our bones.
Those of us who have felt the bombs drop.
Who have cried tear-gas tears.
Filtered thick black smoke through our lungs.
We who have been wounded.
We know, in our muscle memory, what some can afford to deny.
It is not going to be okay; not always.
Neither guaranteed, nor even promised, are the sunny skies of tomorrow.
For yesterday's treasures have turned to dust.
But today…
Today, if we have the opportunity to picnic under sunny skies, it is our right and our responsibility to do so, unabashedly.
To carry this knowledge, with respect, is to love the beauty and the gift of today.
We wounded ones must not search the horizon for warplanes.
Must not grip at the earth in preparation for what could come.
Must not waste today, bracing ourselves for the shock.
There is no such thing as preparing.
As breaking the blow.
As protecting ourselves.

This knowledge can be a cross to bear, or a picnic blanket flung over our shoulders.
Both hold equal weight.
The urgency of loving what is, now, is something the wounded warriors know.
We are not easily subdued or sedated by the common coo of "it's all gonna be okay."
It is not always okay.
We know this.

And, consequently, we also know that the falling bombs kill all things, but one.
Otherwise, we would not be here.
And we know, with ever-valiant tenderness, how precious clear skies are.
So we dance under them when they are granted to us,
Without the torment of what could be, tomorrow.
We love what *is* okay, today.

HEADLIGHTS

I learned of Dominique's death through Facebook. It was Harry's poker night, and I was therefore home alone, covered in paint, blaring music, in my underwear. The news of the world losing this beloved soul floored me. This was before cell phones, at least for the *cavernícolas* that we were, and Harry would be gone late, despite my telepathic efforts to persuade him to cash in his chips and come home.

I was left to process this on my own. And the more I let it sink in, the deeper my heart sank each time the headlights pulling in were not his. From the misfortune of his doing well at the table that night, making it to the final rounds and making me await his return — my terror of losing him growing with every passing hour — the Muse wrought fortune.

We can lose each other at any moment, any of us could be called home at any time...

This piercing fact sucked the breath out of me, and the air that finally relieved my lungs from that asphyxiation arrived, sighing, at the end of a poem, a premonition, a prayer that would oneday be all I had to reference.

From my deathbed in Rishikesh, where most of my words were incoherent if decipherable, I managed somehow to instruct Natalie not only to log into my email and print *Tsunami*, but to read it to me out loud, even though I could not remember what it said. Even though I could not remember my own name...

It had been written for that very moment...

Remind me, Grandmother. I've forgotten again…
How can I sing praises when so much has been taken away?
When all that I have will be taken?
How dare I love wildly, fearlessly, and entirely, when fragility and
impermanence are wound into the bones of every being I will
ever love?
How can I celebrate this moment, when it is turning to smoke
before the candles are lit?
Each breath threatens to be the last, and my foolish lungs insist on
sighing instead of singing,
withering and wailing in discontent,
in poisonous thoughts, trivial worries, petty tantrums, selfish
fears, and unhealed wounds.
Where is Grace, Grandmother?
How can I trust that Grace is here?
When I stumble so clumsily through the passing days, like a
blind, drunken driver in a blizzard, acting as if the roads I choose
do not hurt and do not heal.
How can I believe that we are each in the Great Mother's embrace?
When I am an accomplice to this forgetful belligerence.
When I see so many orphans with no light in their eyes.
Grief-stricken, hopeless, helpless, diseased, empty.
Chiseled and bleeding from stumbling on thin ice,
diminished by injustice, by tragedy, by disappointment and by
stillborn dreams.
How can Grace coexist with such brokenness?
"The sun is always shining radiantly behind the clouds," she says.
It is our limited perspective that casts grey on everything we see.
It is not that Grace is not here, in moments of confusion and
despair.
It is that there are clouds in our retinas, blocking out the truth,
the beauty, the perfection, the color purple.

Sacred heARTwork by: Sarita   145

No shackles of this realm can smother the divine essence,
a flame which is alive and will live on, in you.
The kindling for this eternal fire is the joining of spirits, an
embrace that gives us a little taste of heaven, of home.
It is through loving that our hearts unfold.
Through the unfolding and opening and blossoming of love that
we build something that cannot be taken, not even in a tsunami.
Love is the only treasure worth pursuing.
Only love will not turn to dust, as do our homes, our bodies, our
belongings.
The bonds cultivated, the moments celebrated in companionship,
the acts of generosity and of gentle service, the everyday grati-
tude…all are of an unbreakable substance.
Grace is here.
In sleepwalking and in senseless mourning.
Waiting for a yes.
Yes to today.
To loving wildly, transparently, humbly.
In the storms, she is here.
Grace is a wink between the clouds of this heavy atmosphere.
A kiss blown from the angels that carry them away.
Choose laughter and dancing.
Choose to invite the sunshine in and to allow yourself to be awed,
excited, inspired, and broken open.
Choose to love.
Love all of it.
It is our only true purpose.
To love bravely in the face of vulnerability and danger.
To agree to this dance on thin ice.
To trust that life is tending to the opening of our hearts.
She does this through tiny blessings, through everyday beauty,
and through violent breaking…
She is here, lighting the way to say… YES!
Yes

to love, welling up like a balloon in our chests,
even with the sharp shadow of loss at our heels.
Yes
to living, even when death breathes on our necks.
Yes
to forgiveness and to compassion,
even when others' jagged edges have wounded us and our short-
comings have shorted them.
Yes
to the light.

To basking in it, drinking from it, and weaving with it.
Weaving bridges among us.
Weaving blankets with which to tenderly swaddle one another.

Honor the precious beings that you adore.
Let your heart open,
and open,
and open to them.
Wrap them in light.
Loving is a taste of heaven.
It's our only refuge on this planet of thin ice and tsunamis.
No harm to our flesh can quiet the music that is made in Love's
embrace.
It goes with us.
A happy melody to be hummed with each precious breath.
Breath!
Oh blessed breath of life, be light!

~ 2011

WOUNDED ONE'S PRAYER

Make me an instrument of light as stunning as this darkness.

Make my medicine as potent as this pain.

At least, Great Spirit, be consistent with the intensity of this story; let it continue with as much power and beauty and grace as the one I have survived.

Match the magnitude of my healing with that of my loss.

Teach me the ways of bandaging wounds, of bathing in chamomile, of sharpening the machete and of building the fire. Of listening to the sacred stories, and of testifying to their grotesque beauty.

Teach me to sweat the tears my eyes refuse to release, and to dance the prayers my voice is too broken to speak.

Teach me to take my seat in the council of the initiated, to honor my place in the gathering of the scar clan.

Let the depth of this wound honor the profundity of its origin.

Let my praise be as poignant as my grief.

Let the potency of my suffering translate to unparalleled compassion.

Make of me a home for the displaced,
a shore for the shipwrecked,
a landmark for the lost,
a balm for the broken.

Let my development be a testament to what can take shape in the dark,
Consuelo para los desamparados,

Make me an alchemist, unafraid of melting and shape-shifting.

Teach me to spin tragedy into truth, and belligerence into coherency.

Do not let me fall asleep.

Do not let me waste away in smallness and mediocrity.

Do not let this all be in vain.

Do not let me confuse laying my pain on an altar with placing it on a pedestal.

Protect me from the temptation of sinking, of self medicating, and of losing hope.

Of concluding that this life is in fact wicked, or even worse: that this existence is shallow, or simple.

That it is anything less than a mystery,

anything short of a miracle,

anything other than astounding and magnificent.

Jordyn's little legs dangle over the edge of the fountain. I fish four pennies out of my pocket. One for me, one for Pri, one for Bethany and one for Jordy. Jeremiah doesn't get one, because he would just try to eat it.

"Okay, Everyone," I instruct, in my best nanny voice. "You throw the penny in the water and make a wish." I notice Bethany's eyes narrow with amusement. I have been wishing for nothing but death, and my impulse to lead this activity is out of character, to say the least. I cannot, for the life of me, think of what I might wish for. But I proceed just the same, watching Jordy's eyes widen with attention as she realizes that magic is involved in the small ritual.

This is her first experience with wishing wells, but she catches on quickly. She has watched enough Dragon's Tales and unicorn cartoons to know what making a wish entails. She attempts to close her eyes like in the movies, but her little eyelashes are fluttering wildly with excitement. She places her tiny hand in mine as if this were the way it's always been: she and I, holding hands, making wishes together. And with the unassuming authority that only three-year-olds possess, she speaks the magic words. Words she learned, I can't imagine where.

"Okay, Tita. Close your eyes and wish for all your heart!"

"For ALL my heart!" she repeats, to seal the deal before she releases the penny from her little fist.

"That's right, Jordy," my voice cracks and my eyes sting, out of focus.

"That's a good wish… Let's wish for *all* our heart."

Praise

I DANCED BEFORE I CRAWLED

During my initiation, many mighty mothers took me under their wing. I bow in deep gratitude to all of them, the seen and unseen. This closing portion speaks particularly to my beloved teacher and mentor Melissa Michaels and the Golden Bridge family, who played an indispensable part in my recovery. The following is the Foreword I wrote for the brilliant book Youth On Fire by Melissa Michaels. I share it, both with the intention to give you a glimpse into the powerful work Golden Bridge is doing on the planet, and more importantly, to honor my lineage.

I am no stranger to walking between worlds. Much of my life has been in-between. In-between the continents and cultures that birthed me. In-between the diverse communities that bloomed me.

My bicultural upbringing tuned me in, at a very young age, to the incongruencies, inequalities, and inequities on the planet. I spent much of my young adult life exploring, studying, and ultimately becoming heartbroken by the cracks and the gaps. I came into this work set ablaze with outrage. Haunted by the cries of the voiceless. Tormented by the injustices and in desperate need of support to integrate the weight of the world on my shoulders.

It was in the dance that I began transforming that weight into a gift.

This work is a bridge. And it is a balm. I was initiated through this work, given relevant tools and guidance to resource my passions and direct my call to solidarity and to action in healthy, grounded, life-giving ways.

This work is about mending. Mending the shattered pieces whole again in the ecology of our bodies, our psyches, and our spiritual constellations. Mending the jagged edges of the political, social, and economic unrest dividing our global communities. Mending the places where our modern cultures have forgotten how to hold us as we move through the many passages our mighty and mad lives demand of us.

The old ways of connecting to earth, body, community, and spirit that successfully incubated and initiated our young have been fragmented, diluted, buried, corrupted, and in many cases lost altogether. There is a collective awakening to the need to repair and reinvent what has been lost.

Melissa Michaels, the most valiant visionary I have the privilege of knowing, is on the forefront of that movement. The movement of re-membering these sacred ways.

Melissa dances with the veil, with the mystery, and with spirit, while keeping her feet steady and solid on the ground. Deeply intuitive and attuned, fiercely discerning, and wildly creative, she is an advocate, ally, midwife, and guide. She holds her role with humility and uncompromised integrity, thereby earning the unwavering respect and trust of her community. Over the years she has built a cohesive team around her with impeccable professional skill, precision, and elegance by raising up, as she says, "the children who will raise the children" and by inviting the highest intelligence and deepest wisdom in the room to guide each individual and the whole. The soulful leadership she evokes has created what is simply the most powerful container around.

This work is revolutionary. It awakens the leaders of tomorrow to their innate intelligence, empowering embodied creative expression. It builds common ground and a common language among the Youth On Fire, across the globe. This shared dialect equips each and all with inner resources and self-awareness to move from the center of their own wise bodies and beings out into the world.

This work is life saving. When I was 27 years old, my beloved life partner was killed in a tragic accident while the two of us were guiding a rites of passage journey through the Himalayas. My soul left my body with his. I returned to the dance floor crawling. I was a ghost of myself. My saving grace was this community, and Melissa's commitment to orienting me back towards life. Had the groundwork of my own coming of age in this work not been laid in preparation for this descent, I would not have found my way through.

In a time of utter desolation and disorientation, I was given a map, charting the way home, and the way forward. It helped me to understand the nature of transformational experiences, which includes the hell realms I have traversed. It normalized the groundlessness of thresholds and promised a solid shore on the horizon. It not only gave me hope when I was in darkness, but it gave dignity and nobility to the hero's journey I was on. It gave me a larger picture of myself and my process, and helped me to see that I was not entirely obliterated. Instead, I was liquefying in a chrysalis, creating space for something to re-form, for something new and holy and sacred to be born of the darkness.

I was gifted a space in which I could let it rock without fear. Where I could dive, and exhale, and let it sequence through. Melissa's masterful team gave me permission and confidence to dance with the edge and then rest in the wealth of resources that are cultivated within the circle. Their trust in the process, and in the body/soul's intelligence and ability to heal, allowed me to lean in and trust also. I learned to hold my wounds with reverence and honor, to gently and with diligence excavate my unfathomable pain as a wellspring from which my sacred gifts could be harvested. Alchemizing pain into medicine, spinning sorrow into gold. Taking my place, as a piece in the puzzle, as a part of the whole, as the answer to my own prayers. Finding my home in the very body my soul had fled in the shock and horror I had experienced. Finding my ground where the soles of my feet touch the earth, feeling my pulse in my veins. Discovering and tending to the ember buried beneath the ash. Eventually, even dancing again.

We will never, in our lifetimes, know the full impacts of this work on the world. The ripples created are immeasurable. Each person who has found healing here is a healer in the making. Each young leader awakened is a warrior for change. Each of us, mentored, empowered, inspired by this work, is testament and legacy. The majesty and grace of the global family created beyond all barriers and borders is miracle enough. What each initiate then does in their lifetimes with the power honed here is a mystery that will continue to unfold long after any of us are around to see it.

Words fail us. Miracles refuse to fit into the tight shapes of letters on a page. And yet the aroma alone of this offering is a feast for the hungry. Lean in and get a taste. The power and potential catalyzed is infinite. The breadth and depth of healing is immeasurable.

Your hope for the future just might be restored.

Gracias a la Vida

> " *Gracias a la vida que me ha dado tanto*
> *Me ha dado la risa y me ha dado el llanto.* "

~ *Homero Expósito*

Thank you magnificent soul, for choosing me to sleep next to for the rest of your life.

Thank you big fish, and deep water fish.

Thank you Rainbows for framing Ania's gap tooth smile.

Thank you for Jordyn and her nutcracker ballerina moves, for baby Jeremiah and his wobbly legs. Thank you for abuelitas and their glinting eyes when recounting their mischief and pouring a drink. Thank you niña salvaje.

La que sabe. Thank you Nicaragua, thank you hammock for holding me, and for Pajarito's torta frita on rainy days.

Thank you seawater for salting our rice and beans.

Thank you for coconuts and mangos and plantains and Jacca for falling from the sky.

Thank you Brasil, for cardboard palaces and Circo Sin Fronteras.

Thank you for crystals, and hemp, and Telegraph Avenue.

Thank you for Costa Rica and Boulder.

Thank you drums, and charangos, and syrup in our hearts, arrope de chañar, arrope de algarrobo. Thank you Ivanna, for holding my hand as the bandages were peeled off..

Thank you for machetes and feathers, and fire chains and charcoal eyeliner.

Thank you Kerouac, and Supertramp and Difunta Correa.

Thank you bells and seeds and stones… Thank you for jagged ones and polished ones. Thank you Don Bosco, and mandalas and overly-sweetened yerba for the mate.

Thank you for nepali mustard fields, and jars of honey sent across the ocean.

Thank you for the Maacama bridge, for poo sticks, the Inti Ninjas, the MMMmmmm tribe and the Pluplis.

Thank you Goldilox and Baby Beluga. and Baba Yaga.

Thank you for Bethany, my Gemini twin, my soul mate.

Daddy, my hero.

The mystery, the velvet sky, and wide-winged birds.

Taos, Chai lattes, and cast iron teapots.

Thank you for the blisters on my feet, and the steps they climbed to Machu Picchu. Thank you for the sunrise on the Ganges boat tour. And the grey that gracefully transitioned us through.

Thank you for Xavier's joy in the rainstorm.

For Harry singing at the fire.

For Dwaba's madness. and Raul's compassion.

Thank you for Little Corn Island, for Bridgetts pineapple and for Bronson tapping at my window like Peter Pan.

Thank you for Emerald Ponds, for Rio Quilpo, for Eagle Dance and Liquid Circling. Thank you for Memom's sandwiches, and Pepop's hand in mine. Thank you for Abuela's Nugaton. El uritorco, and Mount Shasta.

Thank you Atlas de Yukuman, and prayer flags & bread crumbs on the path.

Thank you for sobremesa puchitos with Tia Cecilia.

And baths drawn by my cousins using the electric kettle.

Thank you for Rafa's poetry, and Guadi's childlike, green-eyed gaze.

Thank you for dawn, and sleepless nights, and countless restful ones in my lover's arms, and alone. Thank you for el hospital Arcoiris, and the humor it takes to pick the charango with a monkey face. Thank you for phone calls from Maren, and espresso with wine next to Tommy O. Thank you for Honey Walnut Prawns at Fortune with Tomerang.

And Tsing Tao, thank you for Tsing Tao...

And laughter that makes my face hurt.

And Abbey, and Twinkie, and cupcakes from Heather, and care packages from Annie and letters from Cat.

Thank you for Los Zazos. and Vino patero.

Thick throat singing, and drunken brilliant ideas that continue to ring true in the haze of the hangover. Thank you Chaupi, and mazunte, and the sunrise moonset on Punta Cometa with Jimena translating the ocean's song into our ears.

Thank you for long talks in the dark with Daddy on the banks of Lago Atitlan.

Thank you sweat lodge, hot springs, waterfalls, and dust storms.

Thank you Sobonfu for your sisterhood,.

Thank you Melissa, for the seen and unseen.

Thank you Martin, for articulating grief and praise.

Thank you grace, reverence, humility and surrender.

Thank you resilience.

Thank you resilience.

Thank you resilience.

Thank you for butterflies in my belly and elephants on my chest.

Thank you for stowaway love letters in my carry on, and airplane coffee.

Thank you for teaching me to praise life: cruel, beautiful, unimaginable, twisting, turning life.

Thank you Santa Maria & las lobas.

To Clarissa Pinkola, for the scar clan to Shiloh for coloring books, to Memom for majesty...

Thank you Mommy and Amazing Grace, I love you.

And la plazita projected on our living room mirror.

And the perpetual saudade of a Bridger of Worlds.

I love you Marcos Paz, home of innocence and throbbing heartbreak.

Thank you for the Pachamama tree, the Abuela claudia tree, Lolo's Roble, and Grandmother Willow. Gracias Yolandas! Gracias Mariana, por tu valentia y tu voz cantando chacareras!

Thank you big rig trucks, la garganta del diablo, carnavalito, and humitas.

Lavender, Grapefruit and Ylang Ylang.

Frankincense, and the ashby flea market.

Swisher Sweet's and 40 oz'es to Freedom

Butterfly socks and beeswax candles.

Dark chocolate and goji berries.

kombucha and oatmeal stout.

Thank you for anarchist libraries, Ashkenaz, la peña, and surprise magic popcorn in the 3 a.m. VIP. thank you Johannah for the deer antler, and Kanika for the single golden bangle, Thank you Cat for the elixir, and thank you for teepees.

Thank you for the smell of spicy shrimp, and the ring of Luann's laughter.

Thank you for Pri's voice.

for Medialunas con jamon y queso.

Thank you to los Redondos on the radio and four wheel drive.

For Niamfi Frufi, and la Gorda's contagious irreverence. Thank you Gallo for Sineu, los Pereiras for la bailanta, and los termos de Fiamblá. Thanks Lucas for being his brother

Thank you for cocktails in Rachel's pool in Pensacola Florida.

Thank you for Frankie's didgeridoo. for chacareras descalzas, for dulce de membrillo y nueces. For Taliza's bubbles, for Sariah's unruliness.

Thank you for weaving us as one, and shooting stars, and red eclipses, and volcanoes and stardust.

Thank you for the unimaginable vastness, and the humility of this fragility.

Thank you for taking the wheel. Thank you for every close call I was never even aware of, thank you for unlikely conversations, and our power to build Peace.

Thank you to my heart for calling the shots.

Thank you origami cranes and steel drums, and Maya Angelou for "I Rise".

Thank you for Ray Lamontagne, and his big yellow moon over the Greek Theater. Thank you for the Sagebrush of Arroyo Seco, and the smell of Cedar. Thank you for Martha's loving loyalty.

Thank you Pablo for Heartbeats and algarrobo coffee.

Cubanas de ojos azules, and the red bag chicha I never tasted.

The smell of Abuela's kitchen. and the Bugambilia on Abuelo's grave.

Thank you unshakable reflection.

Thank you Eagle of the Himalayas, golden light, burning sun, knees in the sand.

Thank you again, amazing, Amazing Grace…

and Thank you Daddy for rescuing me…every time.

and Harry for loving me…all the time.

Thank you for bare feet on fresh mud, and bats circling our singing.

Thank you for Laurie's banana bread

Thank you for tents set up in A frame houses.

Highway childs, and Troubadours.

Thank you for endless summers, and so much love.

Thank you God, for so much love.

I am blessed, Thank you.

thank you for mohawks, and unapologetic audacity.

Edgy tender succulent nature.

Thank you for Harry.

Gracias mi amor.

Thank you Goddess, for Harry.

I will never question true love…

never, ever, ever again.

Thank you for making me a witness.

For sage copal and palo santo.

Thank you for life.

…and thank you to death for coming for me someday.

Thank you for humanity the sacred and profane.

The guardian angels and angels in disguise.

For music, for acrylics, for pastels, agave, and clay.

For Colibris, for noisy markets, and the chimes of the stupa.
For gongs and cuencos and medicine.
All the medicine, and all the pain that calls me forth to be medicine.
To weave gold from pain…
Thank you for juicy pens, and words that lead the way.
Thank you for guidance and intuition,
messengers and prophets,
for the Holy Spirit speaking through it all.
Speaking through us all.
Thank you for breakthroughs and epiphanies,
thank you for poetry, secret and slam.
Thank you for Wonderland lake, and Cottage lane.
For words and ideas and prayers.
For inspiration, contemplation, for forever lost and found.
For Akhilandeshvari, goddess of all things never not unbroken.
Thank you for fire, for creativity, for hormones and electric skin,
and the dark side of the moon.
Thank you for gratitude, who always wins the battle within, against
all odds, despite logic, and thank you for the way that jade wears us
down like a pumice stone.
Thank for sanity and insanity, complexity and simplicity, for hearts,
heavy, scared and light.
Thank you tribal ouris boris, and for Coyolxauhqui.
Mate con burro, arcayuyo y miel.
Thank you Alice, for your letter. Thank you Lolo for singing in
the choir. Thank you petra for guiding the vision quest, for guiding the healer's and the healing. Thank you to my community
for supporting me always. Thank you for Nama and the babies
picking cherry tomatoes off the vine. Thank you to all of the giants
who have taken me under their wing, and carried me on their
shoulders, and blazed the path.
For divine chaos. For hope. Thank you tormentas eléctricas, and
abuela's flower apron, and alfajores de maicena in spring. Thank

you lechuzas de yerba buena for cheering my pivoting feet, and leading me back to him time and time again.

And jasmine, thank you for the jasmine that continues to grow.

Thank you, naranjo en flor, for only ringing true in the aftermath.

Thank you Frida, for painting your pain, and Mercedes for singing what we feel.

Thank you for Yuko's tea light Earl Grey with honey and cream.

For Sole's pelopincho, for red nail polish, and salta negra en Kilometro 12.

Thank you for Elijah's fervent pacing, the stairs, and the Stony tapes.

Thank you for dolphin Disco, liquid sculptures and Meaghan's Flamenco whaling.

Thank you for the Essex secret gardens, a dog named Harold, and playa Yemanja.

For pillow talks with Peter, and Summer's sweet and spicy pecans.

Thank you for Darling, Darling and Phil's Red Bull in the morning.

Thank you for Iguanas tanning on the roof, and crabs lounging in the bathroom's puddles.

Thank you Akiles, my rontu del Valle, for awakening my bravery, and for not being a killer after all. Thank you for Maggie's soft lap, and Ceci's late night visits. Thank you for Evie, and the beauty of Eve.

For Taliban's pizza casero, and firewood delivered, more precious than roses.

Thank you for Paulina and glitter, and guitarreadas.

For Brother, singing us back to life again. For Ale's picnic baskets, and doorbell deliveries from Blue Bell. Thank you for love notes on bathroom walls, and sidewalk chalk with Jordyn.

Thank you for Rachell's cackle, aguas floridas, and propolis.

For Honeycomb heart, and La cigarra, La maza, and Lila's gotita de Mezcal.

For Semuc Champey and tortillas frescas on the comal.

Thank you for Bridget's gold toothed grin and fresh squeezed pineapple juice.

For lost boys on the train, and found friends around a five dollar pizza.

Thank you stone soup for keeping me honest, and keeping me going.

For liquor store calling cards and lobas around the world. Thank you for the Cosmo's.

Thank you poetizas, cantoras, cuenta cuentos, shamanas, and devadasis.

Thank you for Council, for friends with wisdom, for therapists on speed dial.

Thank you for french toast with Anais, fernet with Fernando, and sloppy cumbia with Lucia.

For hungover humita en olla, your big sister's lipstick, and collared shirts.

Thank you for asados en Mundo Nuevo, and the unconditionality of Clarissa's eyes. For Susy's sfijas, Thank you Techi for giving life to my love. Thank you for aguayos, and tapestries and peyote stitch earrings.

Thank you for Kindling For The Fire, Caminante, La Luna en Ti, Eva Silvestre, Las Fogosas, Creatividad Cíclica, Danzas Ancestrales Luna Silvestre and Puente Pachama.

Thank you for blackouts, and the darkest hour, because you have let me see the dawn, drink the dawn, be drunk by the dawn.

Thank you for miracles, for the grace of God, helping our hearts open and open and open. Thank you for blues swinging on the dance floor, for art walks, gypsy jazz and emoji's. Thank you for Wyoming horizons, angel feathers, and red cowgirl boots. Thank you for rainstorm harmonica symphonies, and love affairs and serenades.

Thank you for packed lunches and Bethany's chicken parmesan recipe being dictated on speaker phone.

For low riders and micheladas.

For consulates and immigration forms that actually lead to freedom.

Thank you for long stretches of highway with my best friend riding shotgun.

For giant flying machines and time travel, world travel, realm travel, and bridges.

For shamanic journeying, and the alchemist's buried treasure in her own backyard.

Thank you for facepaint and gifted wrist bands, for miso soup and violins.

Thank you for the sound of feet on the dance floor, for rhythms and cycles and waves.

Thank you for business meetings at the nail shop, and Fairy Godmothers.

Thank you for the tension that pushes us to resolution, for the burning questions we must live with, and the prayers that help us to do so.

Thank you for universal language, for embodiment, for dance. For Higaion's macrame, and Jennie's fresh mint, and for emptying the jug.

Thank you to love, and to life for sweeping me off my feet, and restoring my experience of magic. Time and time again.

Thank you for burning conversations in the driveway, and for late night journaling.

Thank you to the option of eternal youth, and the promise of death.

For spring, for returning, for butterflies and hummingbirds.

For nectar, for cross pollination, for Persephone.

For the possibility of happiness, because of and despite it all.

Thank you for Utah sunsets, Red Rocks and Gondwana.

Thank you for Mi Guerrero, valiente, tierno, sagrado, entregado. For bringing magic back into my life. For proving to me that hope is never lost. That all ends are followed with a new beginning. For sweeping me off my feet, and giving me ground, giving me home, on this earth again.

Thank you For Jeremiah's drums, and katarina's laughing eyes.

Thank you for the heart of Tafiti- and lava monsters that look just like me.

Thank you for poetry and constellations, for revolutions and bicycles. For Pedaleando America, and Peda-luz. Thank you for Darren's stories, and Abigail's Bump'n Rind, and Mariah's purple hair. Thank you for Savithri's spices, and Dorcus dreaming me to Africa. Thank you for liberation council, for shields, for body drawings, and for the old songs that shake my ribs and the ceiling. Thank you for night bazaars, and Leah's candle, and motherpeace tarot cards in the red tent. For late night calls from kate, and sweet potato fries at Halloween time. Thank you for the chills I get when I hear Coyotes cry. For Shirley's flowering fields, for Lili's cursing, and for la Virgen de Guadalupe. Thank you for paint brushes and fabric, and scissors and glue. For the flowering cactus on my windowsill. For old Ford trucks, and parapentes. For Naomi's words, and wordsmithing, for Freetsie, Tostado and Chango...Sorry, Tootsie, I never did like you much... Thank you for Bartle's deep belly laugh as she reads this. Thank you for Diamonds, and coal, and words never spoken, and words of praise and cariñtos de cosquillita. Thank you for Yuko's hands on my back performing urban exorcisms in the guest bedroom. Thank you for Dave's guitar pick on our coffee table, and Gabriel's jokes. Thank you, Alfonsina Vestida de Mar, for warning me away from the seduction of the waves. Thank you for Los Chalchalerros blaring at 1540 Sarmiento, and Eydie Gorme at 1108, for Pogo con Manu Chau, and milongas "under". Thank you for Silvia's camarones de chipotle, for Mauricio's cleanse on the lawn in Houston, for "Kayla's" French-quarter guardians and Renata's memes. Thank you for saving the twins from separation, and the mystery of their secret language. Thank you for Chacho and his shovel, and Mariana and her garden. Thank you for Courtney in the fig tree and for Cecilita rezando el rosario. For 80 años no son nada, and Jo's I-ching, for runs to the panadería in Tia Elo's baby bus, Julieta's canto lírico and Tio Nico's poetry. Thank you for dolphin lagoons, manglares, ceviche and waves.

For squatters, jugglers, gamblers and fiddlers. For China's candles, and Marla's hands. Thank you for wagon wheel and half-way houses, and Hearth House, and Star House, and the House of the Rising Sun. Thank you for woven baskets, and jean mini skirts. For the gust of wind that blew plastic bags onto Kalpana's terrace. Thank you for wide open spaces, for Humboldt County, and Uncle Gino's strawberry patch. For Música Lijera, and the white steps of Chichicastenango's church. Thank you for the global village that gathered in Yosemite Valley. Thank you for the mighty Jets defeating the Hornets, and la barra brava de River.

For Mosh pits, love letters, Temazcales and Reiki. Thank you PachaMama, Padre Cielo, Hermano Sol y Hermana Luna. gracias por la Lunita Tucumana, For todas mis hermanas lobas. For Lourdes en Aeroparque, for Anita's frascos de mermelada, for Nagchampa and for Harbin with Kat. Thank you for Mira's sheep-skins and for Boleros. For Santana and Santa Claus, for Capoe-ira, grafitti, and free-entry days at the Exploratorium. Thank you to the swans at the Palace of Fine Arts. For satellites, and relics, past, present, future. Thank you for ripples, and spirals, and com-post, and harvests. Thank you for NOW, and for the power of it. For Green Mary, and for BART and for the 51 late night rides. For new year's in Claremont, and for documentaries projected on the plaza's bathroom wall. Thank you for Ribka maya's Borsche, Khambi's green curry, and Juan's jalapeño burgers. Thank you to the white rabbit for making me question reality. Thank you Little Brother for Wish you were here, and Big Brother for three more days, and Kate for loving us, and Juice for forgiveness. Thank you for cave paintings, los sherpas Calchaquíes, la piedra Estebanita, and My family lost and found. Las Mingas de San Marcos, and Katarina's wedding band saving our asses at the Panama border. Thank you for lemon sweet cakes on our winter holiday, For Eddie Vedder and the Beatles. Thank you for redemption song on the boat ride to Isla Ometepe, and the street children of Granada's kindness.

Thank you for every single wrinkle on my face and and salt in my pepper, and song in my heart. Thank you for every soul that has shaped me, touched me, prayed for me, loved me. Thank you for every ounce of love that has moved through me.

Thank you for A-1 market, and Panda's lunch special. For Jahgo-Ma the lime tree, and lemon balm. Thank you for brunch at La Piñata on Sundays, Mimosas and W.B.T.Y.L.P.'s parties. Thank you, Aunt Lettie, for the Daddy song. Thank you for Thanksgiving around the fire, for the pink apartments on Central Ave, for parking lot pajama parties with Jess, for speed walks down Shoreline with Chels. Thank you for all the babies that have been birthed since I saw you last. Thank you for colorful spice rack's, and garlic braids, for aphrodita, and hand scribed recipe books. Thank you for glue guns and needles, and sycquris, and and música andina. Thank you castles made of sand. Thank you for redwoods and mushrooms, and Bobby McGee. Thank you for Mouna's apothecary. For YES rising up in my chest, and NO digging my feet into the ground. Thank you Johnny Cash, and overall-wearing banjo players on the Yuba river. Thank you snail, for the mail. Thank you Tiaki, for seeing. Thank you Laura & Sofia for the Silver Swans, and Brother for being our manager. Thank you for the the crawl, the ashtray, and the Lincoln Park rats and Sundays at la rotonda. Thank you for Loma bola and wild plums. Thank you for Mikey Rat, and for Riff Raff, and for wise men disguised as wingnuts. Bless you. Thank you for the People's park, for Food not Bombs, for Food not Lawns, and for Indie-gogo. Thank you for red refrigerators, and Pollyanna's prisms. For Falcore, and Tia Isabel's family tree. Thank you for the smell of sawdust and merienda coming from Abuelo's woodshop, for the sound of Jordyn and Jeremiah calling for Tita from the top of the big-kid slide. Thank you for breath, for presence, for Joy, for tricksters and for shapeshifters.

Thank you for love rising like a phoenix from my charcoal chest.
Thank you for this blessed life I have been granted.
Thank you.
Thank you for my love, the love that is born of me, the love that flows in my heart, from God, as God, for God… Ashe
Gracias,
Gracias por mi amor, el amor que me nace, el amor que fluye dentro de mi corazón, de Dios, como Dios, para Dios… Amen

A bicultural, trilingual native of both South and North America, and nomad of thirteen years, Sarita is a bridge between the many worlds to which she belongs. 'Kindling for the Fire', a project founded in her belief in creative-expression as a tool to heal, transform, empower and ignite, is the fruit of her lifelong study to what she calls *he*ART *Activism*. Kindling aims to facilitate creative dialogs among people of diverse and often "opposing" backgrounds, therefore weaving a sustaining tapestry of connection and solidarity across the divides.

Sarita is a Ritualist, an International Rites Of Passage Guide, and an Ally to youth from around the world. She is deeply devoted to her sacred and ever expanding relationship to Spirit guiding and inspiring her creative offerings and service.

To connect with Sarita, e-mail her at
SweetWaterTSUNAMI@gmail.com

Also by this author
Caminante: Bridger of Worlds, published in 2008.

Made in the USA
Columbia, SC
03 March 2018